Against the Odds

AGAINST THE ODDS

Harold Mitchell

Foreword by
Brigadier M. J. A. Clarke, M.B.E.

BG

The Book Guild Ltd
Sussex, England

The Book Guild Ltd.
25 High Street,
Lewes, Sussex.

First published 1990

Set in Baskerville
Typesetting by Kudos Graphics
Horsham, West Sussex
Printed in Great Britain by
Antony Rowe Ltd.,
Chippenham, Wiltshire.

British Library Cataloguing in Publication Data
Mitchell, Harold
Against the odds.
1. World War 2. Burma campaign. Armyoperations by Great Britain. Army. Army, Fourteenth
I. Title
940.5425

ISBN 0 86332 476 2

CONTENTS

Foreword by Brigadier M. J.A. Clarke, M.B.E.		6
Prologue		9
1.	The Fly In	11
2.	On to Meiktila	13
3.	Meiktila	20
4.	Defence of Meiktila	25
5.	No Rest	30
6.	Fifth Column and Rescue	46
7.	Stubborn Japs	57
8.	South to Rangoon	71
9.	The Race is On	81
10.	To Rangoon	95
11.	The Start of the Breakout	101
12.	The "Breakout"	109
13.	A Few Escape	121
14.	Massacre	130
15.	Triumph	154
16.	The End	166

FOREWORD

Operational experience in wartime is the experience of a lifetime, the more so for those who are not professional soldiers. Harold Mitchell was a wartime officer commissioned to the Indian Army who was continuously in action throughout the last traumatic six months of the Burma campaign in World War II. He has written from the heart of those times and he has much to tell. His battalion entered the war as part of an airborne brigade to seize the crucial communications point of Meiktila far beyond the Japanese front line. It held Meiktila against desperate counter-attack, broke out to advance on Rangoon in a race against the monsoon, then stood astride the Japanese line of retreat out of Burma and finally established the contact which brought operations to an end.

He has dedicated his book to Infantrymen everywhere. However, the Infantry he knew so well were from the north of an undivided India, Pushtu-speaking Pathans from the North-West Frontier, Mussalmans from what is now Pakistan, Sikhs and Jat Hindus from the present Punjab Province of India. They were all volunteers, unswerving in their oath of allegiance at the time of their enrolment, and in the main from families with a tradition of military service. For their part, the British officers were meticulously impartial in their treatment of the different races and strictly honoured and observed the various religions. The book is a tribute to them and to their successors who have so ably maintained the high standards of the old Indian Army.

The bitterness of the Burma campaign comes through strongly. Japanese generals had unbounded and well–justified faith in the fighting spirit of their soldiers. Bushido, the Samurai code of behaviour of the previous century, had been fostered and preserved, exemplified by the symbolic importance of the sword still carried by officers and warrant officers. Surrender went against all tradition and was unacceptable. The Japanese offensives in 1944 in the Arakan and at Imphal and Kohima had resulted in the most severe defeats ever suffered by the Japanese Army. In 1945, outmanoeuvred in the defence of Central Burma, they fought desperately to extricate the remains of their 15th and 33rd Armies. But the brutality with which the Japanese Army had treated prisoners of war and the civilian population had caused much anger and stimulated the instinct for revenge. At the day of reckoning few prisoners were taken.

This is no dry military history. It is a vivid description of events and a tale worth telling of courage and confusion, humour and hardship, and above all of the loyalty of comrades in arms which should never be forgotten.

Brigadier M. J. A. Clarke, M.B.E.

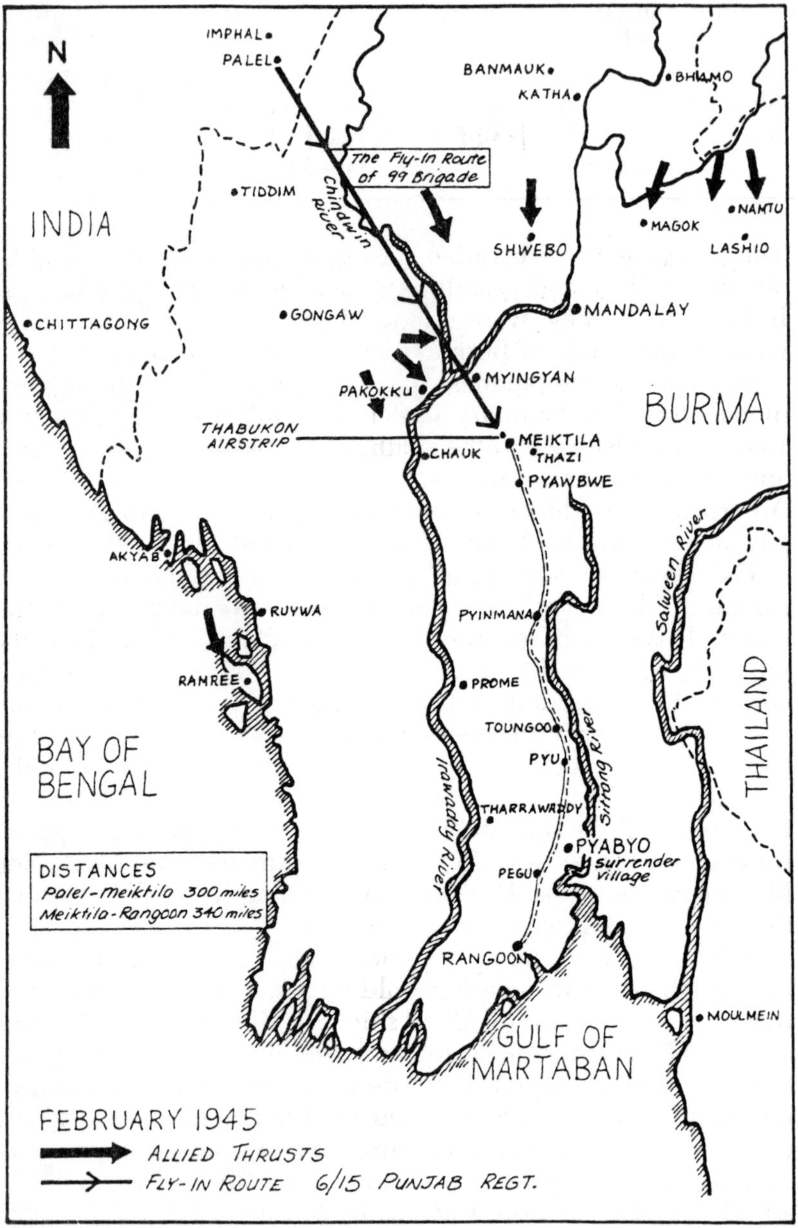
N
IMPHAL
PALEL
BANMAUK
KATHA
BHAMO
The Fly-In Route of 99 Brigade
TIDDIM
Chindwin River
INDIA
SHWEBO
MAGOK
NAMTU
LASHIO
CHITTAGONG
GONGAW
MANDALAY
MYINGYAN
PAKOKKU
BURMA
THABUKON AIRSTRIP
MEIKTILA
THAZI
CHAUK
PYAWBWE
AKYAB
Salween River
RUYWA
PYINMANA
RAMREE
PROME
THAILAND
TOUNGOO
BAY OF BENGAL
PYU
Irawaddy River
Sittang River
THARRAWADDY
PYABYO
surrender village
PEGU
DISTANCES
Palel-Meiktila 300 miles
Meiktila-Rangoon 340 miles
RANGOON
MOULMEIN
GULF OF MARTABAN
FEBRUARY 1945
ALLIED THRUSTS
FLY-IN ROUTE 6/15 PUNJAB REGT.

PROLOGUE

The Japanese Army invaded Burma in December 1941 and by 30 March 1944 had established road blocks north of Imphal, India, where they were defeated. But they still controlled virtually the whole of Burma, and their forces were formidable.

In pursuit of the Japanese, the 14th Army fought through the monsoon and by February 1945 had established bridgeheads at Ramsee and Ru-ywa in the south, at Pakokku in central Burma and at Shebo and Mongwa in the north. General Sultan's American and Chinese Force had captured Bhamo and were advancing towards Mogak, Namtu and Lashio in the north-east.

The Japanese saw large formations approaching the old capital of Mandalay and rushed in reinforcements to meet this threat. This suited General Slim who had planned to draw the Japanese into a fight on the Mandalay Plain, thus creating a corridor for a lightning thrust to Rangoon. The enemy strength at Mandalay was estimated to be six divisions and, therefore, General Slim calculated, South Burma was only weakly held.

Way back in the rear and out of sight, the 17th Indian Division, less one brigade, but with massive armoured support, were preparing to dash forward. The Japanese were watching Mandalay when 17th Division advanced rapidly to Pakokku on their way to Meiktila in central Burma.

14th Army were being supplied from the air, and no other form of an adequate supply would be available until the port of Rangoon was opened to Allied shipping. There were only a few all–weather airstrips in Burma and, therefore, it was imperative that Rangoon be captured before the rains turned the airstrips into lakes of mud. Failure would be a major disaster; a whole army would be without food, ammunition and other essential supplies. General Slim's audacious plan was going well; the advance had been swift, but was it swift enough?

The most forward elements of the 14th Army were in areas

four to five hundred miles from Rangoon. The monsoon was due to start in ten weeks! The task of destroying a tough and resolute opposition, and advancing at the rate of forty-five or so miles in each week, was formidable. 99 brigade of 17th Division, left behind at Palel, India, were waiting to be air transported by the American Air Force to a tiny dust airstrip at Thabutkon, 13 miles west of Meiktila.

What follows is a substantially true account of the vital part played by a brave Punjabi battalion, the 6/15th, raised only in 1941 by Colonel Conner, D.S.O., KPM* in the race against the odds to Rangoon.

The book is dedicated to infantrymen everywhere, who in most wars play a decisive role and are exposed to the highest risks of being wounded or killed.

HAROLD MITCHELL M.B.E.

*Colonel Conner, now 93 and living in Nairobi, was promoted and transferred before the 6/15th Punjab Regiment entered Burma in 1945.

1

THE FLY IN

It was strangely quiet. One moment the noise had been deafening and then the engines stopped suddenly and without warning. As the last propeller feathered to a stop a man emerged from the nearest aircraft and walked to the two British officers who stood nearby. Pulling a packet of cigarettes from his left breast pocket the man spoke with an American drawl, 'O.K. Cap'n, that's the lot and how are your boys?'

'See for yourself,' invited the younger of the army officers.

The three men, an American airforce lieutenant, a major, and a captain, who were British but wore the insignia of the Indian Army, looked toward the soldiers who sat and lay in short rows behind the transport aircraft, one row to each plane.

Had the light been better thirty six Dakotas and six hundred men could have been visible. The men were settling down for the night; their heavy packs, with helmets on top placed in neat rows, together with the boxes of ammunition, picks, shovels and other stores which infantry soldiers normally carry in action.

The quietness was strangely infectious and the three watching officers' voices rose scarcely above a whisper, which was odd. The enemy was hundreds of miles away. A white mist of low clouds came billowing across the air strip towards them and the aircraft were suddenly shrouded in a cloak of feathery whiteness. As the mist was borne softly away on the light breeze the planes reappeared, majestic and bright in the pale moonlight. A new cloud skimmed across the field, hit the nearest plane almost head on and as it split, each half danced lightly along the long fuselage, and milled up and around the tail unit for a brief moment.

The captain shivered. 'I'm going to turn in,' and with his companion walked towards the rows of men who lay quite still.

A sentry standing in the shadow of an aircraft suddenly bellowed, 'Halt!' startling the two officers who quickly gave the password and passed on.

'Hell, my nerves are bloody bad, he frightened me out of my wits,' grumbled the major.

'Nonsense, he would have scared anyone.'

The captain stopped by one of the rows of men, and loosening his boots he stretched himself out on the rough spiky grass, rolled himself in a blanket, and lay with his head cradled in his hands. As he lay looking up at the misty night sky a hundred and one thoughts, a few pleasant, and some happy, but most anxious and urgent came swiftly to his mind. Tomorrow would bring the crucial test.

Except for the prowling silent sentries the 6/15th Punjabis slept, and over their bodies the misty clouds swirled and eddied on their way.

The preparations for battle were completed; the confusion of how and when was over and nothing more could now be done. Long and arduous training periods over rough and tough country were past history. The tedious and hot rail journey from Ranchi to Manipur in a train bursting with mules and men was almost forgotten. The memory of the move up to Imphal in truck convoy driven by Africans which climbed higher and higher into the clouds and moved all the time on the edge of a crumbling precipice still lived.

At Manipur railhead men of a dozen different nationalities rubbed shoulders; where men from England, Scotland, Wales, Ireland, Canada and America, who spoke the same tongue with many accents, mixed freely with Hindus, Sikhs and Muslims from the Punjab and the North West Frontier, all speaking in Urdu language, were well remembered. There, too, were Gurkhas, Chinese and East and West Africans.

The spirit of victory prevailed, in the cherubic smiling Gurkha, in the deceptively carefree attitude of the Yank and Canadian, and in the Britisher there was the quiet confidence of an army on its way to win a war. '*This time*,' they had said, 'we are going to beat the hell out of the Jap!'

2

ON TO MEIKTILA

At 0400 hours 28 February 1945, Reveille sounded loud and clear across the airstrip. The men in the many little rows threw off their blankets and in a few moments the place was a hive of industry.

Men washed quickly, ate a hasty meal, and adjusted their olive green battle dress and fighting equipment. Here and there British officers shaved with difficulty, the absence of light complicating the operation. The air was cool and there was only the low murmur of men until the aircraft engines were started down the line.

In the rear of the seventh aircraft, Vic Lithgow, the adjutant, sat sipping tea from a pint size mug. Nearby stood his orderly, Shamroz Khan, wearing his helmet, and with tommy gun slung over his shoulder. He wore his usual inscrutable expression.

'What's on your mind?' enquired Vic.

'Nothing,' came the reply, with typical abruptness.

'Cheer up Shamroz. We shall be in Rangoon by May and on leave in June,' said Vic. Shamroz kicked the ground with his heel and spoke spiritedly.

'Leave!' he exclaimed, 'Let's chase the little bastards back to Tokyo! Let's grind them into the dust!' Vic grinned.

Shamroz was five feet two inches tall, but his spirit overcame his lack of inches. He was a Khattak*, wore his hair straight and long, and frequently developed an unusually aggressive attitude, particularly with regard to the Jap.

Glancing at his watch Vic fastened his belt, picked up his rifle and walked quickly with Shamroz to the leading plane. As they passed through the battalion the customary greeting 'Salaam

*(Pathan from the N.W. Frontier of India.)

sahib', came frequently from those recognising the adjutant in the dim light.

The engines were making a tremendous din as he and Shamroz dodged the miniature dust storms in the slipstreams of aircraft. Lights were flickering in the recesses of cockpits and fuselages. A jeep bulging with seven or eight aircrew came tearing along, its headlights stabbed the darkness revealing glimpses of the huge planes and the dwarflike men who fussed around them. The jeep skidded to a stop. Two shadowy figures jumped off and the jeep was off to the next plane, and the next, like a bee after honey. Vic looked at his watch. 'Dead on time,' he commented with satisfaction.

Soon, only a few small isolated figures stood about, reluctant it seemed to leave terra firma. Then the second and third planes were moving slowly down the airstrip.

His own party were on board and the pilot stood by the door. 'Good morning captain. Everything O.K.?' he asked cheerfully.

'Yes, fine. Any news from the fighting area?' Vic enquired.

'I'm glad to say that everything is going to schedule, and we have had a good report,' the American lieutenant replied.

There was very little room inside the plane. Boxes of ammunition had been stacked and lashed amidship by expert hands, leaving a narrow gangway of two or three feet down the middle. More stores were firmly secured in the rear of the fuselage and the eighteen N.C.O.s and men sat in two rows facing each other.

'Are you O.K.?' asked the adjutant.

'Everything is O.K.' came the reply in chorus.

'Fasten your belts,' Vic ordered as he and Shamroz took their places.

The engines roared louder now, and then gave a new slightly subdued note as the plane moved gently forward thirty or forty yards, shuddered, and taxied down the strip toward the north. As it moved, Vic looked out of the tiny perspex window toward the runway and saw for a few moments another plane speeding along on its take-off, before its ghostly shadow disappeared into the dusty darkness. The plane swerved violently, steadied itself, and began to move forward, gathering speed rapidly.

The men inside sat still, expressionless. This was a new and frightening experience. Most of them had seldom seen even a motor vehicle or train before volunteering, and now they were belted down in an overladen contraption which as it moved even faster and faster seemed about to disintegrate.

Relief came suddenly as the aircraft floor became level and the plane headed east toward the Jap. Now there was no escape; the men, Americans, an Englishman, Sikhs, Hindoos, and Muslims were irrevocably committed to their destiny, but when belts were released, everybody relaxed. Some settled to doze and others broke into light chatter. In the cockpit, the crew talked in low tones.

'Odd, these Orientals,' mused the American pilot 'They certainly seem to take life much calmer than us, but say, Dick, what are these guys? Muslims or Hindoos? You're the expert.'

The flight sergeant grinned. 'I guess they are a mixed bag. The four with black beards are Sikhs. The ones with the straight long hair, the tough looking types, are Pathans and come, I believe, from up near the North West Frontier. Then the three with high foreheads and short hair are Jat Hindoos, and the two sitting together at the end with features and hair more like ours are Punjabi Mussullmans.'

'That's a lot of nonsense,' exclaimed the pilot, 'I read in the newspaper that after the war they are going to divide India into two countries, one for Hindoos, and one for Muslims because their religions are so differnt that they can't live together. Now you're telling me that back there we've got both Hindoos and Muslims and what about the Sikhs and Pathans, what sort of religion have they got?'

'The Pathans are Muslims but the Sikhs are neither one nor the other.'

'What beats me, if how a handful of Britishers organise these natives and get 'em to fight together against the Japs. When I came out to this goddammed place there was all hell let loose. The natives wrecked railway stations and all the Indians were trying to drive the British out. 'Course,' he continued, and speaking with authority, 'we've had Imphal since then, and if the British hadn't been there the Japs would have captured India and the war would have lasted twenty years instead of ten. India would have become a Japanese colony.'

The navigator stopped working on his maps and chipped in, 'This war out here is certainly phoney. I wouldn't blame the British if they all packed in and went home.'

'Just imagine,' broke in the flight sergeant, 'what a bloody mess there would be in places like Calcutta and Delhi if the Japs ever got that far!'

'I don't know about that,' remarked the pilot quietly. 'From what I can gather there's an awful lot of people in India who would be glad to greet the Nippon; but don't think,' he added quickly, 'that I subscribe to that view. Personally I believe the Britishers have done a lot of good there.'

'How right you are,' a new voice said. It was the army captain, who was squeezing himself into the confined space of the cockpit.

'Well Cap'n, we got a question for you. What are your men, Hindoos or Muslims?'

'Why, both, and some Sikhs,' Vic replied.

'Then how do you account for all this newspaper talk about Hindoos and Muslims not living together? Because if there is anything in it, I don't fancy your chances Cap'n. Dammit, if they can't live together in peace what chance have you got of getting them to live and fight together in battle?'

Vic spoke up, 'It's a lot of nonsense this business of India and Pakistan – I believe that is what they are going to call the new country. It's a sad business,' he continued, 'because in our battalion we have all religions, and all work and play together. There's never any trouble, and if it's possible on a small scale, why not on a large scale?'

'Why not indeed?' commented the pilot.

'Mind you, we have got to watch certain points,' Vic resumed, 'we must be strictly impartial in all ways, and to all classes; each must get a fair deal. At the moment our battalion is a very happy one, and I have no doubt that we will put up a good show.'

'What beats me is how half a dozen British officers train and lead these Indians to fight. After all they have a different language, custom and outlook to us Westerners,' the pilot said looking at Vic, who replied,

'They are all volunteers, and that makes a big difference.'

The pilot and crew busied themselves with instruments and maps whilst Vic gazed intently for signs of movement on the ground below. Dead ahead the sun was slowly ascending above the horizon. The dawn was magnificent. The light came rapidly, and in a few minutes a vast panorama was revealed. Far far away in the distance the sun crept over a range of high blue hills, their outline blurred and indistinct, and which seemed to rise up from a vast yellow table. This was the Burma Plain, and somewhere in it, eighty or so miles ahead the plane would find a tiny airstrip.

Immediately below, and stretching some way ahead was dense jungle, green, matted and seemingly impenetrable. As the sun lit up its upper portion the shadows below became deeper and darker and in greater contrast with the yellow tracks running from west to east. They looked like thin pieces of ribbon. Then the picture was suddenly divided from north to south as the sun gleamed brightly on the Irrawaddy river, which moved slowly and without a ripple towards the sea. Beyond the river lay the plain. In the foreground lay dense jungle.

As the plane crossed the dividing line the first signs of human life were seen, incongruous in the peaceful scene. Smoke rose from half a dozen scattered fires, a cluster of thirty to forty trucks were half hidden in the shadows, and a small group of men were standing on a track with their faces upturned watching the planes which came in single file.

Another smaller river drifted lazily by and then the ground was full of tiny trucks, tanks and tiny men. Away to the right a series of bright flashes indicated artillery fire, and just below a line of tanks in hull down positions were firing at a hidden target. Immediately ahead, a pall of smoke rose vertically from a cluster of houses. As the plane passed over, little figures of men were seen scurrying along a track. Vic got them in his binoculars, 'Japs, and in a hurry too,' he muttered. The navigator looked up from his maps, 'Let's hope the airstrip is clear.'

For a few moments, the four men pondered in silence the possibility of landing in the middle of a scrap.

'Don't worry, Cap'n, they don't know we're coming,' and the pilot laid his arm over Vic's shoulder. 'What matter?' he said, 'For better or for worse, we will land. I doubt very much whether the Jap has cottoned on to what is happening. After all,' he continued, 'this move has been kept pretty secret, and I'm positive the Japs are not expecting a full brigade to touch down in their back yard. This operation takes the cake for audacity. The Imperial Nipponese Army is about to receive the shock of it's life.'

'A lot depends on this op. and if everything goes to plan, and

Meiktila is captured, Rangoon and Burma are wide open to us. Perhaps we will be in Tokyo for Christmas,' chuckled the pilot.

'I'm not so sure about that, it's a hell of a long way off, and in between lie Siam, Malaya, Indo-China, Singapore, and a lot of islands all Jap occupied. It's enough to make the European war look like a picnic. But tell me, what happens to you after this job?' Vic asked.

'Oh, we'll be around for a long time, for more troop carrying and supply drops. I expect we'll meet in Rangoon if not in Tokyo. We are in the plains now,' the pilot gestured downwards. The signs of combat had disappeared and the country was quite different. In striking contrast to the dense green jungles were the gently undulating plains with the yellow earth showing through the scrub, and without sign of house or habitation. The aircrew were searching for landmarks and for Thabutkon airstrip.

The plane penetrated farther into the heart of Burma, gradually losing height, and as it came down to one thousand feet it tossed and wallowed like a small boat in a rough sea. 'I'm going straight in,' the pilot announced. Vic opened the tiny door of the cockpit and was knocked off his balance by the sudden lurch of the plane as it banked steeply. Fastening his belt he shouted, 'When we stop grab your loads and follow me.'

With a sudden bounce the Dakota hit the ground; it rocked as it roared over the rough and sloping airstrip. The soldiers threw off their belts and sat quite still as the plane lost speed. Any moment now the aircraft would stop. It was too late to turn back, and Vic felt his pulse racing and the butterflies in his stomach.

An airman flung open the door; Vic jumped clear and was half blinded by the dust storm caused by moving aircraft in front. In less than two minutes his men had scrambled out and moved at the double for twenty yards, into the cover of the scrub which grew along the edge of the strip.

Two more planes were off-loading and about thirty more were approaching in single file from the west. They were very low and huge, and soon all of them were on their way back to Palel for more troops. The immediate area was reported clear of Japs and the 'build up' of the troops continued quickly without incident. The thirty six planes returned again and again, and by late afternoon the complete brigade, less only a few admin.

troops were in a fairly strong defensive position around the strip. patrols were out in all directions probing up to ten miles.

The night passed without incident and patrol reports were negative. This was odd and perplexing, in view of the proximity of the Japs in force plus the fact that the fly-in could no longer be secret to them, enemy patrols at least had been expected. Had they ventured forth from Meiktila – only thirteen miles distant – and attacked the airstrip in force the subsequent assault on their positions would have certainly been delayed, if not actually cancelled.

A month's delay during this phase of the campaign could have had a most serious detrimental effect, and quite possibly may have turned the ultimate success into dismal defeat and disaster. It seemed that the Imperial Nipponese Army were either frightened or ignorant.

3

MEIKTILA

Just after dawn the overworked and tireless American Air Force returned with more troops, stores and water, and continued flying in supplies until dusk. The day passed quietly until the late morning when two squadrons of Sherman tanks nosed their way along the track which bounded the south side of the airstrip, and halted in the scrub. From the ovenlike cabins of the tanks sweating bereted figures emerged, and one, a lieutenant colonel, hurried off to see the brigadier.

Within a few minutes the tanks were off towards Meiktila. In their wake, over the crest of the rising ground came the infantry, the gunners and the engineers: the 48th and 63rd Indian Infantry Brigades were on the march. Men from Yorkshire, Lancashire, London and the West Country moved forward with Gurkhas, Sikhs, Punjabis and Khattaks, on to Meiktila, and towards the greatest prize of all, Rangoon.

They were out to avenge their 1942 retreat from the capital. They had come back into the heart of Burma in their thousands, resolute and steady, with a smile on their lips, with heads held high, and stout hearts. They came to kill and win, and by the time the sun had slipped down behind the jungle they were at the gates of Meiktila, and ready for a dawn attack.

Sixty miles in their rear at Chauk on the banks of the Irrawaddy, a river four times as broad as the Rhine, and to the south, were large enemy concentrations. In and around Mandalay, eighty miles to the north, six enemy divisions had assembled, and at Myingyan, fifty miles north-west, full scale fighting was in progress. A brilliant piece of strategy had been accomplished. The enemy had been deceived into thinking that the main attack would come from the north; instead his armies had been cut in two by the 17th Indian Division's lightning thrust.

The advance had been rapid, but was it fast enough to ensure the capture of Rangoon before the rains started? Vic pondered on the possibilities as he returned to the battalion H.Q. Tea was being brewed and two short figures crouched over the black tin kettle which was balanced precariously on a pyramid of blazing sticks. Sitting down on a bank in the shade he removed his helmet and wiped the sweat from his forehead and face. 'Hell,' he exclaimed to Peter Reed, the battallion intelligence officer, 'It's hot. I'm not going to last long in this heat Peter.'

'Better than the rains,' Peter replied.

Taking a mug of tea from Shamroz, Vic sat sipping, relaxed, contemplating the lazy peaceful picture. The sun was slipping away, and the shadows growing longer. The air was hot and the earth warm, and for a few minutes no movement disturbed the scene. As he sat watching he thought of the morrow, and cold fear gripped him for a moment. He thought of destruction and death in this foreign land so far from home.

Peter was barely twenty, a theological student. Although he took life seriously, his sense of humour was often apparent. He read his Bible every day; he was a 'sticker', making up for his lack of years by study and hard work. Keen, and in fact fairly experienced by wartime standards, he was only interested in winning the war and getting home again.

His companion, Vic Lithgow, captain and adjutant, was of medium height, wore spectacles and had a soft accent that was unmistakably West Country. An ex-Territorial, he had been called up on 3 September 1939, and was proud of his two years in the ranks where he had served in his native county regiment before accepting a commission and subsequent transfer to the Indian Army.

His interest in Indians and their welfare, and his knack of being able to chat easily with Sepoy, Senior V.C.O., and officer alike created a friendly and respectful attitude towards him by the troops. He and Peter Reed were typical of the British officer who had volunteered to serve with the Indian Army who with the Indian commissioned officers formed the main officer strength.

Only three officers were regulars and held the positions of commanding officer, second in command, and senior company commander. All the rest were young and Vic at twenty-four was the eldest. Apart from the regulars, and two of these were under twenty, the average age of the officers was just over twenty two, not much older than school-boys and yet they held the most responsible task imaginable in leading their men against the enemy. It did not for one moment occur to any of them that they were very young or would fail in their difficult task.

The peace of the hot sultry afternoon was suddenly disturbed by the appearance of the C.O. accompanied by his two Sepoy bodyguard. In a few minutes the 'O' group were sitting on the ground in a semi-circle around the C.O. who sat perched on a tiny folding stool. He gave a slight cough, 'we are about three hundred and fifty miles from Rangoon,' he said. 'The rains will start in early May. Whatever happens we must be in Rangoon before the monsoon, otherwise we shall be bogged down and lose our advantage in armour. Tanks would not be able to move and deadlock might easily follow in bloody awful conditions if we miss the boat. We are being supplied entirely by air, and that applies also to practically the whole of the 14th Army. If we don't get Rangoon and its port facilities before the rains start it's very likely that we shall all perish for lack of food and supplies.'

At the conclusion of the brief meeting, the officers strode off to their companies or units. Major Mike Boon, on his way to Able Company walked a little of the way with Brian Rogers, who commanded Dog Company.

'How are your boys, Brian?' he asked.

'Oh, very fit and raring to go, but I hope something happens soon,' said Brian.

'Yes, we want action soon now, and I don't think we will have to wait too long as there are too many Japs about,' said Mike.

The two majors continued for a few moments in the shadow of some tall bushes before joining their men. Mike, was very tall, fair and upright and looked younger, and perhaps even more boyish than his twenty-three years. Brian was slim and wiry and of medium height. Both had been with the battalion since it was raised in 1941, and each knew every man in his Company by his first name.

Back in H.Q. Shamroz was hanging Vic's mosquito net over a trench about eighteen inches deep, in the bottom of which he had put a layer of dry grass and bracken. A few yards away Vic was completing writing up the war diary, and then went on to read an intelligence report just received from Brigade. The chief clerk Jemadar Bashir Ahmed was typing daily casualty returns, his machine unsteady on a rickety folding table. His assistant, Havildar Kuldeep Singh had just completed his evening toilet, and had wound a piece of cloth around his freshly washed beard. Both the C.O. and the battalion second-in-command were writing letters, Colonel Dick Smedley perched on his tiny stool, and Major Robin London sitting rather more comfortably on a folded blanket placed on the top of an ammunition box. Two sepoys crouched over a small telephone exchange which had been placed in a niche dug from the bank, and nearby the signals officer and members of his platoon were checking and testing portable wireless sets.

Half an hour or so before dusk all ranks of the 6th Punjabis ate a cooked meal prepared in four different Indian cookhouses. The men sat on their haunches eating from their mess tins with chapatis, which are like pancakes in appearance and when half curled in the correct manner serve as knife, fork and spoon.

The officers sat on the grass or boxes, and ate hot stew and drank quite good coffee. Thanks to careful preflight organisation, both beer and whisky were available, and when the officers dispersed to their foxholes, they had eaten reasonably well considering the circumstances. As darkness descended only the quiet buzz of the ever-open telephone exchange and the half-audible whisper of the operators indicated the presence of some nine hundred men, who were manning the positions or resting in absolute silence.

At dawn on the next day, 1 March, the attack was launched. From the east the 255 Tank Brigade blasted its way into the heart of Meiktila; from the west the 63rd Infantry Brigade gradually destroyed the enemy opposition, and from the north-east the battalions of the 48th Infantry Brigade advanced.

By nightfall, over two thousand Japs had been killed, and only a hundred or so had escaped. Those who remained alive were cornered with their backs against the south lake, and were dealt with very effectively on the following morning. In addition to several dumps of ammunition and stores, fifty artillery guns were captured, but of most importance was the strategic advantage gained. A whole British division and a tank brigade were firmly established at Meiktila, an important road and rail junction, which possessed five airfields.

Half of the Japanese Armies were in the north and the other half in the west and south and to them the fall of Meiktila was disastrous.

The 6th Punjabis having been in the reserve 99 brigade during the attack, marched the thirteen miles to take up a position on Meiktila North airstrip, on which American Dakota planes were already off-loading supplies.

As the column approached the town signs of fighting were much in evidence. The enemy positions on the road and in the houses had been blasted almost out of existence. A wooden house leaned crazily at an angle of forty five degrees, one side full of jagged shell and bullet holes, and in the doorway a dead Jap lay on his back, arms outstretched, staring lifelessly toward the clear blue sky. Many more Japanese bodies in bloodstained and ragged clothes lay mangled and shattered by the roadside, providing repugnant evidence of the stubborness of the defence and of the ferocity of the attack. None had been taken prisoner. Our own casualties had been light.

A decisive blow had been struck at the heart of the Japanese Army. It had put fear into the hearts of the Japanese High Command and a song in the hearts of the men of the 14th Army.

4

DEFENCE OF MEIKTILA

Shortly after dawn the battalion moved about eight hundred yards to the north-west corner of the defended area and at once started to dig foxholes and weapon pits at a furious pace. Every man worked as if his life depended on a deep hole in the ground and, indeed, it did. Orders were received to carry out a fighting patrol at first light on the following morning, with tank and air support. B Company were detailed for the job. Speed was essential, for the operation was to be completed in one day. On the following morning the tanks and infantry set off across country, the infantry being carried by the tanks for the first mile and a half.

Two small villages were quickly cleared, during which three Japs were killed, and the column advanced to Tanauggan. Typical of those villages found in the central plain of Burma, Tanauggan was situated astride the main road and consisted of some wooden houses and assorted buildings, and it possessed some considerable strategic value and was occupied by a strong enemy force.

The approach to the village went according to plan. One infantry platoon made a wide detour and took up a position on high ground behind the village, while the tanks and the two other platoons launched an attack from the front. The tanks lumbered along the road, their medium machine guns blazing at the enemy positions, and using with good effect their six pounder guns. The sections of infantry moved slightly in the rear, well deployed, and with their bayonets and grenades winkled out and killed the Japs who were missed by the tanks and who were lying low in their foxholes.

Good progress was made for the first two hundred yards and

the enemy outer defence was penetrated without difficulty. Then the hard core of the position was encountered, and from it came intense machine gun fire and 75 millimetre shells, both with deadly accuracy. From somewhere in the background came a steady screeching stream of 105mm shells to burst with flash and thunder amidst the attacking force. The advance was slowed but did not falter until within one hundred and fifty yards of the centre of the village when the fire-power of the enemy halted both the tanks and infantry.

The initial fighting had been on the outskirts of the village against an enemy in well concealed foxholes and dug-out gun positions; now all the forces are in the village with the exception of the one infantry platoon which is still in position behind the enemy. Every house and hut is defended and every bush contains one or two Japs in holes, five or six feet deep, with a step from which to fire. The battle develops into a number of small actions, with each section of nine or ten men moving forward yard by yard on their bellies, with the tanks giving covering fire from the flanks.

In the close country the tanks are very vulnerable, and having literally carried the infantry into the heart of the battle with hardly any casualties, they are now forced to wait and allow the foot soldiers to make a safe path. The Japs hotly contest every foot of ground, and the men of B Company use every art of their profession and all their daring and courage to make progress.

It is slow and laborious, and the sun now almost immediately overhead burns down relentlessly, parching throats and causing the sweat to ooze and drip unceasingly. The crack of rifle fire, the staccato chatter of machine guns, and the blast and bang of guns and shells continues without pause. A house bursts into flames. Its defenders fight in true Jap tradition, and are burnt alive rather than surrender; soon the odour of their burning flesh mingles with the smell of cordite – acrid, pungent and nauseating.

Yard by yard the Punjabis, grim and determined, push back the equally grim and determined Japanese who, man for man, were not as skilful as their attackers, and who had no room for even local manoeuvre.

B Company kept the initiative; resolutely pressing on, gaining a bit of ground here and a piece there, killing with bayonet and bullet. A section of men choose their objective, perhaps two Japs in a bush, or a machine gun position, and methodically proceed with its elimination. Their Bren light machine gun moves to a flank; two men crawl and dash to cover a few yards ahead. Two more move up, and two more, until the whole section gain perhaps ten or fifteen yards. This procedure is repeated until the heart of the enemy position is within sight and the sweating men flatten themselves in the dust to avoid the continuous hail of bullets which whine and zing around them. Bren guns chatter incessantly in sharp bursts, firing straight into the enemy positions.

John Smythe is some distance from his Headquarters shouting orders to a platoon commander. For a moment his body is hidden behind a cloud of smoke. Suddenly, he wheels and rushes madly to his Headquarters. A flurry of bullets pursues him biting into the dust feet at his heels. But death and the Jap machine gunners are cheated as John flings himself into cover and panting hard, struggles to find a handkerchief. His left arm is bleeding and hanging limp. His face is wet with sweat. Feverishly he mops his face whilst his orderly ties a field dressing over the hole on his bicep.

Another one hundred and fifty yards advance is slowly made but at around midday, it seems as if nothing can shift the Japs, and the two forces are locked together with barely a few yards separating their advanced elements.

The sun is right overhead now and the men who had been fighting for four hours are hot, and their throats parched. Their faces are covered with thick, sweat-soaked dust. Some, in good cover, use their water bottles and spit out mouthfuls of dust, water and white saliva; others in exposed positions dare not move and just lie and wait and watch.

The firing has stopped and there is a queer uncertain silence. No-one moves. Nothing stirs except the dying embers of the burning house. Suddenly a Jap sniper spots a target. His shot is returned twenty-fold and the noise of firing rages once again.

John talks by wireless to his platoon which went around to the rear of the enemy position. In Urdu he gives his orders.

'I want you to advance from the north. When you are within charging distance of the village fire your Very pistol. We will give covering fire and then attack with you.'

The minutes pass slowly and there is now only spasmodic firing. The men nearby fidget uneasily. John gives the order to advance, stands up and peers through the bushes.

'They will take about fifteen minutes,' he says softly to Robin London who has now joined company headquarters.

The noise of firing rises and falls, mostly by rifles but now and then a Bren gunner tested his weapon. The two officers talk in low tones as they look toward the Jap position and then at their watches. The expected time of action comes and goes and ten minutes drag by.

'Where the hell is Jemadar Lal Khan?' John demanded impatiently.

The words were barely spoken when the Very signal went up and cascades down in a shower of ruby crystals. Every weapon fires at once and then stops. There is a shout from some way off and then more shouts follow and war cries can be heard.

John moves forward with his two platoons. The enemy are suddenly looking in both directions and the pace quickens. All the men with John hurry forward and from the flanks the tanks are pouring streams of bullets right into the heart of the enemy position. Suddenly, they stop and a voice bellows 'Charge!' and the sixty soldiers attack with bayonets. Through thick prickly bushes, through houses and sheds they rush forward, bayonets flash and the grenades rumble as they burst in foxholes. On they storm killing all in their path with a sure, unnerving accuracy.

Then quite quickly and almost unexpectedly it is over. The two attacking forces have met, and the sweating tired soldiers reform and count the dead. The end and victory came so quickly that it was hard to understand the slowness of the initial advance.

John's casualties totalled five killed and seven wounded, but he is satisfied. His battered Stetson hat is perched on the back of his head and his neckerchief is like a wet rag. His face is covered with a thick layer of dust and on each cheek there is a thin vertical line of pink. John's face is always pink. He mops his forehead continuously with a sweat-soaked handkerchief, and his uniform clings to his plump body.

His companion, Robin London, a little older, perhaps about thirty, is slim and neat. His beret sits nicely on his head at just the right angle, and his uniform is smart. He is Irish; John is Scottish, and in every other way too they are quite different, but together, with the Tank officer, they have achieved success. John stands up and pulls his uniform into shape. His left arm is tucked inside his tunic.

In the vicinity of the Jap H.Q. bodies lay in various positions. It is estimated that a further one hundred and fifty were in the outskirts of the village and the booty, in addition to swords and odds and ends, included 9×75 mm guns, 1×105 mm gun and four machines guns. A party of Japs, perhaps twenty or thirty strong had escaped.

The Punjabis of B Company and the Deccan Horse Tanks were jubilant. A Jap force in a fortified position had been attacked and soundly defeated, and pleasure turned to pride when it was learned later that the enemy belonged to the Japanese 18th Division who were recognised as the elite of the Nipponese Imperial Army, enjoying a reputation similar to that of the British Brigade of Guards.

The battalion had registered a victory, a victory which set the standard for the battles to come. It was fitting that Vic was able to publish a message from the divisional commander, which included the words:-

'You have captured Meiktila, a vital bastion of the enemy defensive and maintenance layout. The enemy garrison was strong in numbers and fought fanatically. The fighting spirit displayed by all ranks, intimate co-operation, and mutual confidence were the factors which won the day. Well done.'

5

NO REST

During the following week, only one infantry company remained at the base at a time, and with M.T. drivers, clerks and medical orderlies, worked from dawn to dusk improving the defences. A small amount of barbed wire became available and was laid fairly loosely in zig-zag fashion about fifteen inches high, and almost concealed in long grass.

Since the whole division was still being supplied by air, and aircraft were still very scarce, no other artificial defensive aid, or even sufficient wire was available. Fortunately, the battalion area was very small, being approximately two hundred yards square, including a Field Ambulance Unit, and part of Brigade Headquarters, who were also occupying a portion of the 'box' perimeter. Punjis (sharpened bamboos fixed at an angle) were fixed in profusion in front of, and in, the wire and trip wires and booby traps were laid across all the likely approaches. Digging became almost an obsession, and sections vied one with another to achieve the most efficient shell-proof shelters. A room four yards wide by about seven long was constructed underground with anti-blast walls around the entrance, and this proved ideal for conferences and the officers mess. It was six paces from the outer perimenter. Its roof was flat at ground level, and consisted of a good five feet of earth supported by stout lengths of timber which had been acquired locally.

Water was now being obtained locally, which was fortunate, for the heat caused a constant thirst. 'V' cigarettes, obnoxious weeds of very doubtful origin, began to arrive with the rations, and because of their inferior quality were in plentiful supply, but better brands and good quality pipe tobacco soon became available in small quantities.

Enemy activity was almost negligible, but two Japs who approached a road block died from unnatural causes, and about half a dozen Japs fired rather indiscriminately from long range at the battalion position for twenty minutes or so without drawing fire. Enemy bombers on two or three nights circled for about an hour before dropping a few bombs, which caused casualties to a light ack-ack unit which formed the only defence against air attack. It appeared that the Jap was carrying out his reconnaissance by means of a number of patrols each consisting of half a dozen men, and who had no great difficulty in eluding our own patrols which were clearly not sufficient to cover the fairly close country which lay to the immediate north of Meiktila.

One evening a copy of a letter from the Commander Corps to G.O.C. 17th Indian Division was received. It read:

> 'Now that you have completed your mopping-up I would like all ranks to know what a good show they have put up, and how your success and theirs is looked upon with pride by myself and the whole of the rest of the corps. You have given the Jap the worst knock I have known him to get in the past two years. This has been done by the splendid spirit and determination to get in and get at the Jap wherever and whenever met. That is the way to deal with the little swine. May your good hunting continue till we have driven him right out of Burma.'

On 10 March, the battalion received orders to set up a base at a point some fifteen miles due east and to patrol the area from there. Moving across country on a compass bearing and carrying rations for forty-eight hours, the H.Q. and two companies covered the distance in just under five hours. The countryside was flat and almost bare; little grew on it except a few trees and patches of very prickly scrub.

The battalion set up their base under a large shady tree a hundred yards beyond the Rangoon-Mandalay railway line, and at first light company patrols set out to the north and east. The constant searching of the villages failed to produce any sign of the enemy, and orders were received from brigade to continue for a further four days, and to indent for air supplies. Apparently, the experts in air supply allowed for a twenty percent wastage or thereabouts, on the assumption that this amount would fall into enemy hands, or be irrecoverable owing to the terrain.

Neither condition prevailed and the lone American Dakota swooped gracefully and very low over the dropping zone. In its open fuselage doorway a man leaned casually; he waved and kicked out the bundles of supplies, and was last seen still leaning against the door support as the plane made off for its base at Imphal. It was all so very easy and simple, here, right in the heart of enemy occupied Burma, the Dakota, unarmed and unescorted, flew at ease in safety.

The rations, of American origin and most attractively packed, were better than expected and contained canned fruit, dried meat and vegetables, cartons of chocolate, matches, cigarettes, salt, mepacrin, and vitamin tablets, boiled sweets, and biscuits, plus a fairly large drum of rum. In fact, everything to provide a balanced diet for a limited period. With water obtained from a nearby uninhabited village, the party were adequately fed even though fresh bread, meat and vegetables were sorely missed.

The weather was almost unbearably hot and the necessary movement on foot across country for distances of up to ten miles at a time was exhausting, and salt intake in the form of dissolved tablets was essential. This, in addition to taking mepacrin at dusk and vitamin tablets during the day, all ranks drank salt water just after dawn. The absence of heat exhaustion, debility and malaria reflected credit on the unit's medical discipline.

On the morning of the seventh day, the battalion, less one rifle company, were ordered to return at once to Meiktila where it was urgently required. Within half an hour B Company, together with main H.Q. departed, leaving behind a Rear H.Q. and the Mortar Platoon with Vic in charge. Arrangements were made for the rear party to set out for Meiktila early on the following morning.

As the first rays of light crept over the hills, Vic tried to contact Brigade H.Q. by wireless. Quietly at first, and then as the minutes passed without a flicker of an answering call, his voice became louder and his calls more urgent.

'Damn and blast,' he swore, as Major Douglas, Charlie Company, came hurriedly into the H.Q. and said briskly, 'We are ready to go.'

'I know,' replied Vic, 'but I want to get an all clear from

Brigade. Its some time since we had news about the area between here and Meiktila.'

'We want to cover as much ground as possible before the sun becomes too hot,' said Doug.

'Well, you can be getting ready and meanwhile I'll give Brigade another five minutes,' Vic answered.

Doug stamped off to collect his company and in less than five minutes was back with rifle slung over his shoulder ready to march. A few yards behind him Terry Lord of the Mortar Platoon sauntered at a leisurely pace and with a carefree and an almost benign expression on his round plump face. He and Doug watched Vic calling Brigade H.Q. and as they stood there in the very early morning light, the contrast between them was most marked. Doug was slight, sharp featured, blue eyed, with a somewhat fussy and worried manner which was sometimes irritating to his companions. Conscientious to the nth degree he never seemed to relax, was a total abstainer and a good man, much respected by all ranks.

The other, Terry Lord, was quite the opposite. He turned the scales at sixteen stone, but he was not fat and his fitness was remarkable. He never fussed or bothered and was always ready for a joke, an attitude easily misinterpreted as irresponsible by those who failed to penetrate beneath his carefree veneer. In fact, under his supervision, the mortar platoon had reached a high peak of efficiency, and his conduct on patrol in a previous campaign had been acknowledged by a Mention in Despatches. He and Vic were good friends.

Brigade H.Q. became audible and as Vic waited for the brigade major to come to the set, Terry remarked, 'Next time we come out we'll bring some carrier pigeons.'

'Just as quick as this bloody thing,' muttered Vic, turning back to the set. 'This is Apple Number Six speaking. We are about to start. Have you any information? Over.'

'Your message received. No information. Over,' came the surprisingly clear reply.

'What about the area between us and you. Is it clear? Over.'

'No enemy activity. What time will you arrive? Over.'

'At 1100 hours.'

Vic scrambled hurriedly to his feet, saying, 'O.K. let's be off. It's now just on six, we will march for three hours and then halt for ten minutes.'

'Right,' replied Doug, 'That will take us to the temple just south of Ohshitkin. Will you bring up the rear?'

Well dispersed, the body of some one hundred and fifty men maintained a cracking pace for three hours, and arrived at the appointed halt with a few minutes in hand, and just as the sun was becoming hot.

The 'temple' consisted of only a stone pillar about two feet square and three high, standing in the shadow of half a dozen trees which grew in isolation on a small plain. The leading company avoided crossing the open ground and halted in the cover of the thick scrub some three hundred yards to the north or on the right of the temple which was surrounded by flat neglected paddy fields. Vic and his party, bringing up the rear of the main party, halted near the edge of the scrub on the east or near side of the temple. Terry mopped his brow.

'Thank God we've broken the back of the march,' he said.

They were about to loosen their equipment and sit down for ten minutes when a sentry casually drew their attention to a soldier who, carrying a rifle and clad in green battledress, was running like a rabbit, zig-zagging, and covering the rough open ground at an amazing speed. Terry and Vic watched him for a few seconds in complete astonishment. His uniform was the same shade of green as their own.

'Christ, it's a Jap,' exclaimed Vic. 'Get him.'

Half a dozen riflemen fired almost simultaneously at the target crossing their front at ninety yards range. The Jap sprawled headlong on the ground as if hit, then was up and running again as fast as ever towards the cover of the trees into which he disappeared.

'Give us covering fire,' Vic shouted to his rear section, adding, 'Come on Terry, let's go.'

With rifles and tommy guns at the ready the two sections advanced towards where the Jap had gone, and when they had moved about thirty yards another amazing sight appeared. The heads and shoulders of twenty or so Japs popped up in a small group from behind a waist high bank which ran out from the trees on the near side. Vic rapped, 'We'll attack, keep over to the right and get in the trees.'

The two officers and sixteen men broke into a fast trot, riflemen fixing bayonets on the move, and tommy gunners with their weapons ready. The decision to attack had been instinctive, without time to think or ponder. The enemy were barely a stones throw away and behind cover while Vic and his men were on open ground. There was no choice of action. They covered another twenty yards before the Japs opened fire with a dozen badly aimed rifle shots.

'By God, they're windy,' thought Vic as he yelled, 'Charge.'

A burst of fire came from their left rear as his supporting section gave cover; the pace quickened and it seemed that a bloody hand-to-hand fight was about to take place, when, with only a few yards between friend and foe, the Japs turned about and fled as fast as they could go into the scrub. Vic was surprised, and surprised again to find newly dug trenches under the trees. He and his men quickly occupied the position as the sound of heavy small arms fire came from their right rear. 'C Company in action too,' said Vic to himself. His reserve section were already making their way across the open ground.

'Get under cover,' he shouted, and no sooner had the men scrambled into the trenches when rapid fire from three enemy light machine guns swept the position from the left. A storm of bullets whistled and thudded into the trees, some hit the stone pillar and ricocheted in all directions. The men ducked, but in a moment or so they started to fire back deliberately and with careful aim. They had one Bren light machine gun and the Orderlies, Shamroz and Safar both opened fire with their tommy guns. The Japs stopped firing and Vic was able to have a good look at the enemy.

Their numbers had increased; now there were about two hundred, some lying on the ground a hundred yards away and the rest standing in cover at varying distances up to three hundred yards. 'This is it,' Vic thought, and sweat began to pour from every pore and he felt his pulse racing.

'Plenty of targets, Sahib,' Shamroz murmured almost gleefully.

Vic's calm returned and his brain began to work again. Twenty one against two hundred, ammo limited, C Company (his only support) already in action four or five hundred yards away, and in between, the open ground, which the Japs had now covered by fire.

There was more spasmodic firing from the rear.

'Open up the wireless. Get Charlie Company. You and you move over there to the right and aim low. Shamroz and Safar get behind that stone, one each side, and watch that bit of dead ground.' The orders came rapidly and the men rushed to obey.

An earth bank which formed the edge of a rice field ran obliquely across their front no more than fifteen yards away. 'If they get behind that in force, we are sunk,' thought Vic as he moved over to Safar and Shamroz. 'Watch that bank.'

'Aim at their stomachs and don't miss,' he ordered.

Shamroz and Safar, both short and stocky knelt behind the temple stone, one on either side, their eyes intent on the bank in front, to which the leading Japs were now moving. Seven or eight moved ahead of the main body who halted two hundred yards away obviously waiting for a signal from their forward group who dashed and crawled quickly from cover to cover.

'Get them in that open bit,' Vic said and moved to look at his left section. He had just scrambled behind a tree when the section leader rushed towards him, 'Lord Sahib marna walla (Lord Sahib is dead). Look, Sahib,' he said with panic in his voice. Vic looked and moved involuntarily and oblivious to the bullets which were zinging past him, in the direction of Terry Lord who lay ten paces away from the left tree. He lay behind a small bank of earth which gave no adequate cover to his massive bulk. To his left a Sepoy lay motionless and lifeless, and on his right and rear, three more Sepoys lay still, their weapons still clasped tightly.

Vic moved and the section leader grabbed his arm, 'No, Sahib, wait, wait.' The words penetrated Vic's brain and he stood still behind the tree, and for a few moments he felt and knew an indescribable fear as the strength left his body, leaving him weak and dazed. All feeling left his legs and stomach, departing in a giddy tumult. His thoughts detached themselves. He was elsewhere.

The section leader shouted twice, 'Look Sahib, over there, over there!'

Vic was again in full possession of his faculties. 'Hells bells,' he exclaimed as he saw six Japs lying behind the bank barely twenty yards away, their heads out of sight but their legs visible, and unseen by Vic's men who were in the trenches. He pulled out two grenades from his hip haversack and placed them gently on the ground.

'When I move out in the open aim a burst at their legs,' he shouted.

Vic looked at Shamroz and shouted, 'Keep your heads down' and stepped out from behind the tree with a grenade in each hand. Two Japs raised thir heads; one received a bullet in the face, which dropped from view as Vic tossed the first grenade underarm, gently. One – two – he counted. On three, the second grenade had gone, and he was back behind the tree when the first grenade exploded followed almost instantly by the second.

The position was suddenly clouded with smoke and dust and in a moment of wild anxiety Vic wondered if he had missed the target and if the Japs would charge unseen, but there was no need for alarm for as the dust drifted and visibility returned, there was no movement behind the bank, and judging from the positions of the Japs' nether portions, little life.

Vic wanted to make sure, so putting a foot in his companion's cupped hands, he swung up to a branch from which he could see the ground behind the bank. Six Japs were sprawled in a heap with legs and arms sticking out haphazardly, and the heads of two a mangled mess.

Three Japs broke from the far cover and dashed towards the near bank. They had covered half the distance when two sharp bursts of tommy gun fire came from Shamroz and Safar. The leading Jap stumbled drunkenly, crashed to the ground and over his crumpled body the second Jap collapsed, writhed and lay still. The last member of that brave little group was hit in the throat and for a few seconds his lifeless body ran around in a circle before the uncanny motive power spent its force and his body subsided into an untidy heap.

Vic was reminded of an incident in his youth when he saw a chicken beheaded; it too ran after death. Now he felt strong and almost happy. He laughed loud and heartily. He glanced at his watch: only ten minutes had passed since he had occupied the position. He looked around and a flame of exultation surged up within him as his eyes saw the dead Japs. He thought, 'We'll beat them yet.'

No Japs were now within a hundred yards where their bodies formed little blocks of shadows in the scrub, their courage perhaps a little daunted by the fate of their comrades. It was only a question of minutes before they would attack again.

Vic moved quickly to each man in turn and found them all in a cheerful, aggressive mood as he cautioned them against wasting ammunition. He reached the left flank and studied his dead and wounded lying out in the open and realised he must get them back quickly.

The farthest body lay fifteen yards from cover, the nearest about seven yards, and whilst he planned a method of getting them back into relative safety, Terry moved. Vic blinked and then grinned. 'He's only wounded,' he exclaimed, and the message went from man to man along the line. Three men instantly volunteered to bring him in.

'No,' replied Vic, 'not yet, better find where the machine guns are first. Jemadar Sahib,' turning to the Mortar V.C.O., 'watch that dark patch over there as I push this hat out.' He knew the dark patch hid the machine guns one hundred and twenty yards away on the left.

Lying behind a bank he edges himself along and when he is within a yard from the end, he slowly pushes his hat, balanced on the end of his rifle, out into the open. A sudden flurry of bullets hit the ground, kicking up spurts of dust a yard or so beyond the hat, which he withdraws, and then pushes it out again. The sharp rat-tat-tat of the light machine gun starts again and continued for a few seconds. Vic glances over his shoulder and sees the Jemadar taking aim, his body tucked away behind a tree. He fires ten rounds rapidly and then two more in quick succession.

'O.K. Sahib, it's gone,' the Jemadar shouts, and when Vic looks again, the dark patch is flattened; only dead Japs remain. Vic moves back into a trench and then scrambles to his feet as a shout comes from his right. A dozen or more Japs have moved to within fifty yards of the position and are working quickly forward. Vic feels himself go hot and cold.

'Hold your fire, tommygunners, the rest pick your targets,' he shouts.

His heart is thumping madly but his confidence had fully returned and he took careful aim at a Jap head which protrudes above cover. His shot starts an exchange of fire; forty or fifty rifles cracked again and again; another Jap machine gun chatters incessantly spewing bullets at the handful of men who stand firm in the trenches. The sweat pours down Vic's face. The smell of cordite and dust nearly choked him, but his head is clear. Suddenly, the firing ceases, and when the dust and smoke had cleared, no live Japs are nearer than eighty yards, except for six who, in the confusion of the firing, have gained the cover of the bank twenty yards away.

Shamroz and Safar watched with their guns ready and eyes fixed on the bank, waiting absolutely motionless for the Japs to appear. There is an indescribable silence; both enemy and friend watch each other. The six Japs have to move backwards or forwards. Both directions are across open ground. If they succeeded in coming forward into Vic's position with grenades, they can possibly create sufficient havoc to allow their comrades to charge in force.

Clearly, they are fanatics, but their presence so near is dangerous, and they must be killed and quickly. The fate of Vic and his men hung on a slender thread. In the background he can see the Japs moving forward slowly. Two rifle barrels creep slowly over the top of the near bank, but no hand or head becomes visible. He looks at the tommy gunners, and sees Shamroz blink. His heart is thumping. His eyes returned to the Japanese who are moving slowly forward through the scrub, the sun glinting on their weapons. He can see the sights on the enemy rifle barrels on the near bank.

The silence and tension is almost unbearable. Then suddenly, the six Japanese appear from behind the bank. Instantly, the tommygunners open fire. Two of the enemy fall at once, and the other four, hit in several places, seemed to hesitate before disappearing, but none get over the bank and the main body, having seen the failure of the attempt to rush the position, halt, still a hundred yards from the temple.

'Phew, that was near,' Vic breathes his relief, looking at the enemy through his binoculars. He can see their features quite clearly. They seemed only a few yards away and he is puzzled by their smart and clean appearance. This is no party of enemy on the run, but a well turned out and equipped force who, for a reason which Vic cannot fathom, are reluctant to attack in force. They could easily have surrounded the temple and picked the defenders off piece-meal, or charged with rifle and bayonet. Either course could only end in success for them, but Vic can see no sign of any preparation.

The Japanese, spread out on a front of a hundred yards, lie in ones and twos, and quite still. There are no gestures or the sound of orders being given. It is uncanny.

Vic speaks to the wireless operator. 'Try and contact C Company again.'

'No use, Sahib, their set is not open.'

If only C Company would move four hundred yards toward them they could drive the Japs off and get Terry back. Then he has another idea.

'Try and get brigade or battalion H.Q.,' he orders. 'I'll get some artillery down, or some smoke.'

No reply comes, not even a distorted crackle or faint whisper.

He stands for a few moments waiting for a quiet spell between the firing which was being maintained spasmodically in both directions. Then, putting his hands to his mouth, he shouts, 'Cee Company,' in his loudest voice. No answer comes. He shouts twice more, and when his eyes search the scrub some three hundred yards away, he sees quite distinctly the shapes of men half hidden in the shadows, but no answering call comes.

With lips set, face grim and sweat-lined, and feeling the heavy weight of his responsibility, he thinks deeply for some plan of escape. He must delay the attack and get help from C Company who were one hundred strong. Suddenly he shouts, 'I want a volunteer to run to C Company and get help.'

Two men reply immediately.

'I'm going to take a party out on the right flank to divert the Japs' attention. When we start firing, run like hell to Douglas Sahib. Tell him we need help quickly. I'll take you six out on the right in two groups of three to that big tree. O.K.?'

Vic took the Bren gun and with two sepoys dashed quickly to a point twenty five yards away. The other group runs forward to the tree, and as soon as they are in position, Vic and his party join them. The Japs were now much better targets, and exposed to flanking fire.

'Fire,' he bellowed.

At about fifty yards, with big targets bunched together, the first fusilade was devastating and the Japs are clearly surprised. About a dozen cease to take any further interest in the proceedings and the rest hurriedly move their positions. But one, a major, stands up and with raised sword rushes towards Vic's little party. The sepoys opened fire, Vic tilts the Bren gun and squeezed the trigger and more by luck than judgement, several bullets hit the major in the head. He dies instantly.

Out of the corner of his eye, Vic sees the volunteer scampering over the open ground to the rear and he gives a sigh of relief. As the firing stops, he says, 'Right, let's go back as we came. Keep on firing.'

In a minute or so the party are back in their position and Vic is relieved to see Terry, the wounded sepoys and the three dead, lying in cover of the low ground behind the trees. 'Well done,' he cries clasping Jemadar's hand with both his own. He bends over Terry who is, surprisingly, conscious.

'Don't leave me Vic,' he almost cries, 'it was hell out there.'

It's all over now. We'll get you out of here in no time,' says Vic soothingly.

He bends to examine Terry's wounds and is shaken when he realises their extent. One elbow has been smashed, two bullets have entered the stomach, and a bullet is embedded deep in his right thigh.

'Here, take some morphia,' he says.

Terry loses consciousness and Vic, with the help of a sepoy, dresses the wounds, carefully washing off the dirt and blood. He applies field dressings and put the damaged arm in a rough splint made from two fairly straight sticks. The job is heavy going and Vic sweats profusely as he and the sepoy handled Terry's sixteen stone. As they laboured hurriedly in the broiling sun, Terry's eyes opened.

'Don't leave me, Vic, don't leave me,' he begs plaintively.

Vic reassures him and finishing off the bandaging, washed Terry's face and hands.

'I'm in hellish pain, Vic. Give me some more morphia, and for God's sake, some water.'

Terry's cry is heartbreaking and Vic wishes he can grant the request, but instead he wetted Tery's lips.

'I'm sorry Terry, but no morphia for an hour, and no water.'

'Don't give him water,' he says to the sepoy, 'if you do, he'll die with those stomach wounds.'

Terry's eyes are appealing and he cries desperately, 'Vic, I must have water, I'm parched. Just a drop, please.' His voice trails away in a whisper as he loses consciousness.

Vic shakes his head and moves over to attend to the other wounded who fortunately are in much less serious condition. One has a broken leg, the other a bullet in his posterior, and both are made reasonably comfortable.

Spasmodic firing has continued during this period, and Vic moves over to the left flank. The Japs are again advancing and his heart sinks as his imagination conjures up an allout Jap attack which must surely lead to the annihilation of his party. After holding out for more than an hour and a half, it would be bitter if defeat came now. There was Terry too, whose removal to a place of safety is of vital importance. Ammunition is now getting very low, and most men are down to less than a dozen rounds.

The Japs seem just as numerous despite their losses of thirty or forty, and as Vic contemplates the situation, it seems quite hopeless. He began to despair of ever getting Terry away. His heart sinks and he feels despondency heavier and deeper than he had ever felt before. Firing continues, but not on a heavy scale and the Jap shooting is inaccurate and no one has been hit since the first assault.

Their tactics seemed odd for during the battle they have not evolved any sort of plan whatsoever to dispose of an enemy force which they outnumbered by more than twenty to one. As Vic ponders, he is more and more puzzled.

Shamroz and Safar are still kneeling almost motionless behind the pillar and only move to shoot at a Jap who appears from behind the bank. This seems a satisfactory and safe arrangement to Vic and he makes a quick dash back to the wounded.

Terry again urges Vic not to leave him and becomes very agitated, 'If they attack for God's sake shoot me,' he cries.

'Don't talk such bloody nonsense,' replies Vic abruptly.

About one hundred and fifty yards to the rear C Company lay dispersed. Vic stood up and beckoned them on.

'Try to get them on the wireless.' The operator gave a gesture of despair. 'Sahib, I've been trying all the time, but

I don't get any reply.'

Obviously C Company thought that the ground in between the two positions was covered by fire, but if that was the case, why in hell did they not go around their left flank, Vic thinks to himself, frustration and fury boiling within him. He walks to the front trench from where he watches the front for twenty minutes. He fires about ten times at Japs in the rear and at roughly ninety yards range. He examines the result through binoculars and reckoned that there are at least half a dozen less to cope with.

A sepoy points to Terry, who is calling, 'For God's sake give me some water.' Terry's cry goes to Vic's heart, and he feels a spasm of anguish like a knife thrust in his body.

'You can have a drop Terry, but you have a stomach wound and water can be fatal in this heat.'

'I don't mind dying Vic, but I must have water,' Terry says desperately.

He lies there in terrible pain, his face ashen and drawn, his mouth and lips parched and his body soaked in perspiration. His thin wet uniform clings to his skin. Vic felt awful. Water could kill Terry, yet his condition and pain tears at Vic's heart and he feels utterly helpless.

'Water, water,' Terry's voice comes weak and plaintive.

Vic gives him three sips, washes his face and neck and adjusts his bandages. Intent on making Terry comfortable, he forgets for the moment his other problems.

Going back to the forward trench he prepares to advance on the right front to divert the Japs and drive them back. As he turns to give final orders his spirits soar, for across the open ground in the rear, a platoon of C Company are approaching. In a few moments Vic is giving fresh orders. Three light machine guns are soon strafing the Japs, who withdraw rapidly. Major Douglas and the rest of C Company arrive almost immediately.

Two platoons advance and the enemy move back and around to the east and stop almost half a mile away. At first some have the temerity to stand about in the open but go to ground quickly when two snipers open fire.

A stretcher is hurriedly made from two branches and a blanket, and the dead are buried. Several officers' swords, a flag, and documents are taken from the enemy bodies which lay in a jumbled and bloody mess behind the bank.

At 12.30 the party moves off, with Vic a few yards behind. The going is slow, walking being difficult over the paddy fields, and the speed is regulated by the stretcher party who frequently have to halt and change sides or members. During one of these halts, Vic is able to contact base by wireless and arrange for an ambulance to come at once.

For some time, the Japs move on both sides at four or five hundred yards range, and now and then a bullet whines across the open ground through the middle of which Doug and Vic had decided to advance.

After an hour and a half, they reached closer country and a track which leads almost straight to Meiktila. Here the ambulance meets them and in twenty minutes or so Vic and the wounded are in the battalion position which also houses the Field Ambulance Unit.

After his report had been made he washed, removed nearly ten days' growth of beard and put on clean uniform. For an hour he busied himself with his normal routine duties and after tea walked over to the Ambulance Unit. In a few minutes Vic was standing beside Terry's bed. Terry, to Vic's surprise and embarrassment, grasped his hand and said, 'Thanks for what you did Vic, I thought I was going to die a dozen times.'

'Nonsense,' said Vic, 'How do you feel?' he asked.

Terry grinned, 'I never thought that a bed could be so comfortable.'

He was clearly half under the influence of drugs but he was cheerful and apart from his pale face looked reasonably well. For a few minutes they conversed in undertones, until the colonel appeared.

'Not too much captain, he's had more than enough for one day,' he said quietly.

Vic and the colonel bade Terry goodnight and walked together to the door of the tented hospital.

'What will happen to him?' asked Vic.

'We can't move him, so we will have to operate here, tomorrow, about midday.'

Vic walked the few yards to the battalion command post and his trench, where Shamroz, his tough and inscrutable

Pathan was being sick. He looked very ill, and Vic was alarmed.

'What's the matter?' he enquired anxiously.

'Nothing, Sahib. It's only the blood. There was a lot of blood,' he said sadly in a broken voice between retches. Vic, whose own stomach was sensitive, fought down with difficulty a similar impulse and put an arm on Shamroz's shoulder. In a minute or two Shamroz had recovered.

'What happened to the booty?' Vic asked.

'I've put the sword and flag in the command post. Here are two pistols. Can I keep one?' Shamroz asked hopefully.

'Which one?'

Shamroz produced another from his pocket. It was a .38 automatic, beautifully made and perfectly balanced.

'You picked the best,' Vic said.

Shamroz shrugged resignedly. 'I killed a lot of Japs today, Sahib,' he said simply.

'You did very well. I'm going to bed. Goodnight,' Vic suddenly felt overcome with a heavy weariness. As he lay down, he fell asleep.

6

FIFTH COLUMN AND RESCUE

Vic was awakened by Shamroz with a mug of strong tea. He sipped it slowly and let the effect of the beautiful morning dwell in his mind and body. The air was fresh and clean and only slightly warmed by the morning sun, and taking deep long breaths, Vic felt a strong sense of well-being, of health and strength.

The long sleep too had refreshed him, and it was good to be alive. Then remembering Terry, he started to dress, and was fumbling on one knee for his boots when the shelling started. The sudden blast knocked him down on to the earth which rose and fell like the swell of the sea. His head became a giddy tumult and he saw a thousand stars. His ears hummed a high pitched note until his hands instinctively sheltered them from the deafening explosions.

Then everything became quiet and he lay in the trench paralysed with fright, trembling from head to toe and covered in dust. Presently, he stood up and with shaking hands hurriedly finished dressing. He had barely finished when the shelling began again, causing his nerves to jump in all directions and his heart to thud like a drum. This time the shells were more scattered, and fifty or more yards in the rear they exploded harmlessly on open ground.

Further shelling continued at irregular intervals during the morning, and it was obvious that the enemy had the position under close observation. To everyone's relief, it ceased around midday.

During the night the Japs had seized the airstrip and had dug in on the east side, from where they could cover most of the strip by small arms fire. A detachment of the R.A.F. Regiment held the west side, and the 6th Punjabis received orders to destroy the Japs. Two companies with tank support, attacked. Within two hours the enemy were beating a hasty retreat leaving a score of dead in the bushes and foxholes. Overhead a dozen Dakotas circled anxiously waiting for the all-clear signal to land. They could not wait much longer.

An enemy operation order captured the previous day by another unit revealed that a special task force of a thousand commando-type troops had been ordered to capture and hold the airstrip. But the most significant and interesting part of the order related to the enemy rendezvous. This was at 0900 hours on the previous day and at the temple south of Ohshitkin village where Vic's party had halted. The subsequent battle had without doubt shaken the Jap considerably, and accounted for their half-hearted attempt to hold the airstrip.

Their orders did not include any attack other than against the airstrip and this omission explained their lack of a plan to attack Vic's party but Vic felt that the information regarding the enemy rendezvous should have been passed to him before his party's return from the patrol base to Meiktila. He had asked for information and the reply had been negative. He was angry about it and made his views known to all concerned.

Vic was on his way to the mess when Major Robin London, the battalion second in command, waylaid him.

'I have some bad news for you. Terry Lord died under the operation,' he said.

Vic had not even contemplated that Terry would not live, and the news stunned him.

'Come on, you had better have a drink.'
Robin took Vic's arm as they made their way to the mess. Shaken to the very core of his being and with heavy heart, Vic gulped a peg of neat brandy, and wiped the sweat from his face.

'I can't believe it,' he muttered to himself. 'I saw him last night and he looked fine.'

The funeral took place on the following day with as much ceremony as the situation permitted. There was a strange atmosphere at the graveside, almost, it seemed to Vic, of conspiracy combined with furtiveness. He and Major London had driven from the perimeter during a lull in the enemy shelling which had recommenced at dawn and continued, with frequent intervals, until well into the morning.

At the graveside the firing party had already assembled. A padre was waiting and there were a few other soldiers waiting around and who, apparently, were not sure whether they were part of the ceremony or not. The service was brief and several times the padre's voice was drowned by the thunder of artillery. The ground where they stood trembled twice and bits of loose earth tumbled on to Terry's blanket shroud as it lay in the bottom of the shallow trench. The firing party from Terry's own platoon was unrehearsed and not sure of the drill, but they fired the final salute in a competent manner. The padre moved a few feet and started the next ceremony as two men began to shovel the earth into Terry's grave.

His death was a grevious blow and all hearts were sad, but such are the fortunes of war, and as the days passed hearts hardened and there was no further outward sign of sorrow, but in silent thought he was often remembered.

During the next night a party of a hundred Japs occupied the north portion of the airstrip, and their removal became a matter of extreme urgency for not only was it necessary to retain the strip for the landing of essential supplies but badly needed reinforcements were expected to arrive by air. No planes could land whilst the enemy remained.

Destroy the Jap at once. The order came at dawn and two companies with tank support launched a vicious attack. The encounter, fierce and brief, was over by midday, and the strip, now back in Allied hands, began to function. The weight of tank and machine gun fire combined with grim determined infantry soon had the Japs reeling, and the few who escaped death fled like frightened chickens to the safety of the open countryside.

The Khattak Company, still on the roving patrol, killed two Japanese in a village twenty miles east of Meiktila, reported their own casualties as two wounded and requested their evacuation. There was no road or track to the village and Vic, as adjutant, found himself in some difficulty. Robin London came to his rescue and approached Brigade H.Q. Soon a light aircraft was on its way, carrying mail and supplies, and the wounded were soon in the Field Ambulance.

The Japs resumed the bombardment the following morning, and the battalion received its first casualty from shell fire. One shell landed right on the edge of a slit trench and within a foot of its unlucky occupant who was in a crouching position and below the level of the shell's point of explosion. To this fact, the sepoy owed his life, but he was badly shocked. Emerging from the cloud of dust, demented and screaming, he ran round and round the position for five minutes eluding all attempts at capture until mercifully, he collapsed unconscious.

Seeing one of their comrades affected in such a manner was an unnerving experience for the onlookers and Vic, barely twenty yards away, felt the blood drain from his face. His body trembled. 'Poor devil,' he said softly to Shamroz, who had dived for cover into Vic's trench. Another salvo of shells whistled over followed by odd ones and twos every few minutes for an hour or so.

This harrassing fire was a nuisance and at times alarming but everyone soon became accustomed to it, and by careful planning of their movements, particularly with regard to avoiding the few open spaces no further casualities occurred. All ranks quickly learned to keep within diving range of a hole and since the actual defences now resembled a rabbit warren, this was not difficult. If anyone had to cross an open space, it paid to wait until after a shell had fallen and then move.

Initially, all ranks were afraid of appearing afraid, but after a few officers had made some undignified rushes for cover, the importance of putting on a bold front was soon forgotten. At breakfast, the shells were not even mentioned, but the few officers who sat at the improvised table cursed at their rotten luck because Cologne had fallen to the Allies almost on the same day as Meiktila and the Air Mail edition of the English paper, which had just arrived, devoted almost the whole of the front page to Cologne, and only a paragraph to Meiktila at the bottom of an inside page.

'Anyone would think that the capture of Cologne was more important than the fall of Meiktila,' grumbled an officer.

'So it is' said Vic. 'The sooner the Germans are defeated the sooner all those well equipped divisions will be able to come out and win the war for us.'

Time did not permit further discussion and after the meal of beans and tinned bacon had been completed, there was a rapid dispersal.

Later in the day, two companies of the West Yorkshire Regiment took over the perimeter defences and the battalion came under command of 9 Brigade of the 5th Indian Division for the night, but early on the following morning the battalion reverted to the direct control of 17th Indian Division. Since the West Yorks had arrived, it was expected, quite naturally, that the battalion would move, perhaps to attack the Japs responsible for the shelling, whom it was generally thought were preparing to attack Meiktila. As anticipated, a warning order to move to an undisclosed destination was received from Brigade at about 1145 hours. An hour later, when preparations for the move had been completed, the order was cancelled.

The move eventually took place on the next day, with sections of men in single file, well dispersed, to the divisional artillery 'box' which was situated about a mile to the rear. Three shells exploded one after the other and right in the middle of the marching men a quarter of an hour after they started. There was a rapid opening of ranks and the battalion wheeled left and resumed marching. Five minutes later four shells fell among men of the leading company. The men cursed aloud and at length, and again there was a change in direction and the pace increased, but the shells came again and again and as the battalion arrived at the artillery 'box' a salvo of shells fell astride the rows of men, followed by another and another as the companies took up their positions for the night.

Two sepoys were killed outright and five severely wounded. The rest were shaken and angry. It was obvious that since the battalion had moved across country, which was not visible to any Japanese positions, someone, probably a local, was directing the enemy fire from inside Meiktila itself!

The accuracy of the shelling had been uncanny. At one time there seemed to be no escape from the explosions; there were no convenient foxholes to provide safety and the men felt like hunted animals. They swore vengeance and meant it. Had the fifth columnist been found he or she would have been torn to pieces within seconds.

The battalion set about its new task of providing protection for the artillery who were of course of vital importance and hitherto had manned their own defences. Now that the enemy was becoming more aggressive at fairly close range, adequate protection was necessary.

At first light A Company moved to patrol the area north west of Meiktila and, in particular, the wooded slopes which ran down to a large lake. The Sikhs were always in form on this sort of task, and they found the Japs within an hour. At first, there were only a few odd rifle shots from the bushes which grew at the bottom of the slope. The Sikhs probed forward up the middle and on the flanks. They discovered that the enemy positions were only lightly held so Major Mike Boon decided to attack and then carry on with the task of locating the Japanese main position. The forward Japs were soon dealt with, but behind and on a forward slope was a strongly fortified position complete with 75mm and heavy machine guns.

These, apparently, were the Japs who intended to recapture Meiktila. They did not appreciate the Sikhs' visit to their position, and as their outer defences were overrun, they opened fire. For a few minutes all hell was let loose as rifles and machine guns vied with one another to kill the Sikhs. The leading men were pinned down at short range; four were killed and eleven wounded immediately, and among the latter were two who could not crawl or walk away.

Sepoy Kartar Singh was slightly ahead of his comrades, and had been scrambling for cover when a shell landed within a few feet. He felt no pain when a large splinter entered his thigh, shattering the bone and tearing the flesh. Smaller pieces pierced the muscles of both legs. He immediately lost consciousness and fell as if dead. His comrade, Taza Singh, saw Kartar crumple, and disregarding the bullets and shells which whined past, started to dash to Kartar's aid, but before he had moved two paces, a Jap machine gunner caught him. He staggered drunkenly, and fell, and as he writhed in agony, felt that his legs were being cut to pieces with a hot knife. He could not see the gashes in his thigh but felt the pain, excruciating and bitter.

He struggled against the darkness which slowly closed over him, but he fought in vain and in a few moments the movements of his arms ceased; his body gave a violent shudder and he lay still. His lungs tremoured as they fought for air and the two men now lay unconscious twenty yards or so in front of their comrades, covered by heavy enemy fire. Immediately, efforts were made to bring them back to safety but after the sixth attempt to rescue them, and when two more men had been wounded, Mike Boon was forced to take the toughest of all decisions. There was no alternative and the two badly wounded were left helpless, lying under the Burma sun.

The Japs were obviously in great strength. An attacking force of one company would be mown down like grass before the scythe, and Mike felt he could not risk more lives in trying to save two, precious though they were. Perhaps after dark there might be a chance. So A Company withdrew, man by man, moving from cover to cover, crawling along the gulleys and dashing over the bits of high ground; every movement bringing a fusilade of bullets, but at one hundred yards a man who suddenly appears and runs for six paces and then is gone from sight, is a difficult target.

Once the Sikhs had arrived in good solid cover, five or six hundred yards from the Jap, the precautions were relaxed, and they moved quickly in sections back to the battalion H.Q. where Mike reported to the C.O. His information was both good and sad. The news about the enemy fortified position was welcomed, and Colonel Smedley promised that should conditions be favourable, a rescue attempt would be carried out after nightfall.

It was almost six o'clock when Kartar Singh became conscious. The sun was on its downward path to the west, and its rays shone across the lake creating a myriad of dancing mirrors. His crumpled figure stirred slightly; his eyelids twitched, and nervously he rubbed his eyes, gently and very slowly. He was tired and weak, and he instinctively lay quite still, wondering, as his senses and memory slowly returned. His head ached, and it seemed as though a hammer was thumping inside his forehead. For a minute or two he lay struggling silently against his weakness, and the daze and dizziness which swirled around and up and down in his head.

Slowly the mist cleared and he remembered the attack, and thinking that it was still in progress, he cautiously raised his head and looked towards the Jap position, but it was in deep shadow, and he could only see the trees and undergrowth merging into the darkness of the slope. Everything was silent and still. There was no movement anywhere, and he frowned, puzzled. We were advancing he thought. What has happened? Where is my company? He turned his head and saw the dancing mirrors on the lake, and the sun going down.

He almost cried out in pain for as he took stock of his surroundings, he tried to move his legs. Perspiration ran down his face, his head reeled, as he struggled against another wave of unconsciousness. He became aware of his parched throat and tongue, rough and dry as sandpaper. Feverishly, he fumbled for water, the fingers of the right hand clumsy and shaking as they worked to loosen the carrier straps. The exertion was exhausting; he gulped for air several times between bouts of heavy panting, his chest and stomach heaving. Then he became dizzy again and almost lost consciousness. His head went round and round like a whirlpool as he fought to hold the ebbing strength which flowed in and out of his body. He rested oblivious to time and danger reaching into the very depths of his being to gather strength.

Twenty minutes went by and still no movement came from his bloody and torn body. Then it stirred, the right hand slowly moved down to the water, deliberately as if mechanically controlled until it stopped abruptly and rested still on the bottle. Fingers slowly closed around the neck, the knuckles showing almost white through their dark skin. He tipped the bottle and allowed the water to run around his mouth, over his tongue and through his teeth, collecting the sticky white saliva until he spat it out. A few drops dribbled down his chin and on to his beard as he drank noisily in gulps until the bottle was half empty. The water warmed by the sun hardly quenched his thirst but it gave him strength and lifted the cloud from his mind.

His position suddenly became clear, he was alone, half-helpless, forgotten, wounded. The Japs would come with bayonets. Death would be bitter. They would torture. The thoughts flashed, giving him release from bodily pain, and easing the throbbing of his temple. Calmer now, he thought of escape and his fingers searched for the holes in his legs. Contact with the wounds started a wave of heat which sped up his spine and lingered around his neck and head. Hot and exhausted he rested for a few minutes, and then, with legs still, twisted himself carefully around, every inch an effort, and looked behind.

Taza, huddled but alive, appeared dimly behind a bush ten paces to the right. Kartar stared, focussing his wavering eyes and wondered. He looked harder and recognition came. Taza signalled, pointing to the sun, lowered his hand, pointed it backwards, pointed it at Kartar, then at himself, and grinned, white teeth flashing. Kartar understood, and nodded twice, then rested, his head screwed around watching Taza. After dark, they would move. Both men knew that the Japs were barely two hundred yards away, and likely to come out at any time.

Major Mike Boon and his senior Subedar, Harnham Singh, sat between two large slabs of granite which served as company H.Q., and talked anxiously in low tones. Harnham was elderly, probably much too old for active service, but he was fit, active and much too proud of himself and his Sikhs to ask for an easier job in a peace station. His thick beard was heavily tinged with grey, and his lined kindly old face gave him an appearance of a Father Christmas. He ruled his Sikh 'sons' as he called them, firmly and fairly.

'I've got some volunteers, Sahib, to bring them in, and if the Colonel Sahib agrees, I'll go too,' he said in his soft voice.

'How many men have you got?' Mike asked.

Harnham hesitated, 'Well, they all want to go, but I've picked twenty, Sahib.'

'Too many!' replied Mike quickly. 'A smaller party will have a much better chance. Let me see, yes, four men for the stretchers, and four for their relief and protection. Pick out eight, with a good N.C.O.'

Colonel Smedley watched as they moved out in single file until the last man had disappeared into the dark of the night. He stood alone for a moment, then turned about, and strode to his bivouac, his face set and anxious.

The news had spread rapidly from trench to trench, from Sikh to Muslim, to Hindu, through the rifle companies to the H.Q., the admin. units, and to the Madrasi fitters. 'Taza and Kardar were left behind, badly wounded, near the Japs. A patrol is going out to rescue them.' The words were spoken softly, received almost reverently, and passed on.

A blanket of gloom settled on the battalion as it moved silently into position for the night. Every man was ready to volunteer for the patrol; every man knew about Japanese atrocities, their cruelty and their treatment of prisoners.

The patrol moved swiftly and in dead silence for about a mile, their dark figures in single file, concealed in the shadow, their steps surefooted on the uneven ground. Presently, they halted in the dark shadow of a clump of bushes and in whispers made their final plan to rescue the men.

Some distance ahead, Taza and Kartar had made strenuous efforts to move, and in great pain had gained a few yards. In so doing, they had avoided capture.

A few minutes after the sun went down behind the trees

which grew on the edge of the lake, Taza had beckoned. Kartar, who had lain quite motionless for several hours, started to turn his shattered legs. The pain ripped through his body and he gripped the grass hard, fighting to remain conscious. His head reeled, the ground rose up and down, and the bushes behind which he sheltered swayed sideways. He struggled against oblivion, pain and exhaustion. Summoning his courage and willpower, he pulled himself along the grass with his hands, pausing after two or three pulls to recover. He made slow progress; his legs were useless, and ached from groin to knee as if being cut with a jagged knife. With every heave forward came confidence and hope. The pain seemed to lessen as he joined Taza, who whispered, 'Come this way, over to the low ground where we can hide.'

They made towards a clump of thick bushes growing in a natural depression. Silent except for their heavy breathing, and the quiet swish of the grass, they covered twenty yards in about as many minutes; then, within a pace of the cover and temporary safety, Taza stopped suddenly and lay with his body and face pressed flat and hard against the ground, motionless. Kartar coming up in the rear with his head down, his mind intent only on reaching cover, missed Taza's boots by inches, and became aware that someone was coming. A twig cracked, there was the murmur of subdued voices. Kartar froze, heart thumping. The voices came from the north, from the Japs. There was a shuffle in the undergrowth and a faint rustle. The two men lay still and rigid with fright awaiting the rush of feet and the inevitable bayonet. The voices lingered, subdued. Death was but a few paces away.

There was then a louder voice and the Japs, having apparently finished their searching, moved off. Kartar bumped his fist on Taza's legs, 'Go on, go on,' he whispered urgently. Taza wriggled into the bush, scratching face and hands on the sharp thorns, and Kartar quickly pulled himself alongside his comrade. Utterly exhausted and quivering with fear, they lay side by side and like two hunted animals, nestled together for comfort and succour.

Some four hundred yards to their rear, the rescue party watched the Jap patrol file slowly past. Clearly they were being careless, thought the rescue leader, and with regret, restrained himself from carrying out an attack. It would be easy, a man for each Jap, and with surprise in their favour, the Sikhs could throttle the lot in less than five minutes, but one shout and the Jap main defences would be alerted and the rescue attempt foiled.

Two men with stretchers remained well concealed at the rendezvous, and the N.C.O. with six sepoys moved towards the enemy position. For perhaps three hundred yards they were reasonably safe, provided no noise warned the Japs. When they reached the dangerous high ground, they started their arduous crawl. Before each movement, careful fingers searched the ground ahead for twigs which might break and bring down a hail of bullets. Almost an hour passed before the patrol neared Taza and Kartar.

The awful despair which had shrouded their minds when the Japs approached had gone; hope of escape was uppermost in their minds. In whispers they discused a route to safety. Suddenly, there was a bird call, 'Eek, eek, eek.' Startled, they trembled with fright. The call came again, nearer this time, then from only the other side of the bush the call came quickly. It was human. Kartar whispered, 'It's our brothers come to save us.'

'Eek, eek, eek,' he called presently, his voice weak and fluttery, and in a few seconds they were being carried on broad backs to safety. It was a swift, bumpy and painful ride hastened by a fusilade of fire from the Japs as the patrol neared the dead ground.

Their spirits and stomachs uplifted, and warmed by doses of strong rum, the wounded men were carried through the trees and into the safety of the battalion perimeter, where Captain Deitra, the medical officer, was waiting with morphia. In a trice, Taza and Kartar were drifting peacefully away into a state of blessed oblivion.

The 'Doc' dressed their wounds. A Bengali, youngish but with a lined and tired face which seemed always to be about to break into a smile, he was popular and much respected. He worked fast with a sure and confident touch.

7

STUBBORN JAPS

Shortly before dawn on 21 March the battalion trekked back to its former position on the north west corner of the Meiktila defensive position. The area was now appropriately named 'Thunder Box' and a salvo of shells greeted the unit.

For the first time since the fly-in all ranks were able to relax for a reasonable period, to do their laundry, and make and mend. By just after ten o'clock, the bushes in the rear of the perimeter were festooned with green socks, shirts, trousers, tunics, and greenish underwear. The latter were 'battalion dyed,' and it was clear that the standard of dyeing from khaki to green was not high. Nevertheless, the resultant colour was satisfactory from the camouflage aspect, although somewhat streaky when hung out to dry, and not at all regimental.

Vic strolled around the position and made his way to Brigade H.Q. to find out how the West Yorks were faring. The news was bad; there had been casualties and no progress was being made against the Jap who were firmly entrenched. There was a frustrated impatient atmosphere in the building which resembled a dutch barn and in which Brigade H.Q. staff lived and directed operations.

Due perhaps to the unusual amount of leisure which officers were enjoying, the mess was full when Vic entered. A discussion on the situation was in progress and opinions were being expressed on the coming of the rains, and whether the division would get to Rangoon before the monsoon started. Rangoon was still three hundred and forty miles away, and no-one knew how many Japs would be met on the way down the road, and how many battles would be fought before the division started to move south. Meiktila was more or less surrounded, and the date was 21 March. The monsoon was due to start during the first week in May and it seldom failed to arrive on time. Seven weeks in which to cover over three hundred miles; countless Japs all over the place and more expected from the north; thousands more between Meiktila and Rangoon, and a considerable enemy movement from west to east in the area south of Meiktila.

The task seemed quite impossible. There was every reason to prevent the capture of Rangoon during the dry season, yet in some strange manner no-one seriously believed that the campaign would fail and everybody, despite the arguments against, took success for granted. Failure was not even contemplated.

The meal of canned peas and meat and dehydrated potatoes was nearly over when a message from Brigade H.Q. put an end to conjecture, and ordered the battalion to move on at first light the following morning with the objective of attacking the Japs who were occupying a village about four miles east of Meiktila.

Fifteen miles to the east, Brian Rogers and his company of Khattaks were busy in an apparently strange manner. A casual observer, if there had been one, would doubtless have thought that the hot sun was at last having some effect on the men who sat or lay on both sides of the railway lines forming two half circles. There was half an hour's daylight left and the men appeared to be resting, but Brian was moving from group to group, giving instructions. A complete section of the down railway line was missing.

The odd sight was easily explained. The railway was the main line from Mandalay to Rangoon and it had been reported that when the line was unguarded a train, full of enemy troops, had escaped south to Rangoon. Mandalay, seventy miles to the north, was at the time still Jap occupied and it was presumed that the trainload of troops was a part of their withdrawal and according to Intelligence it had passed through the area during the night after the battalion had withdrawn from the same area on 15 March.

Until reports of the train were received, no watch had been kept on the line which had been badly damaged in places by American bombers. Then, apparently, a minor miracle had taken place. The damage had been repaired overnight and several hundred Japs had escaped by the simple method of catching a train to Rangoon, or at least, to a point further south of Meiktila.

Consternation had been evident in certain high quarters, and Brian who had that day received the information, together with a message that more trains were expected, had taken steps to ensure a derailment. Now he was taking action to dispose of the Japs who might not be killed in the expected crash. When his dispositions were completed he sat and waited.

He had removed a piece of the line in such a place that any train coming from the north would, with reasonable luck, topple over and off the embankment, rendering the occupants incapable of resisting the small arms fire which, guided by the light of Very cartridges, would pour in from both sides. So he and his men rested, lying on the still warm hard earth for hour after hour, quiet, still and alert, with ears strained for the rumble of a train.

Several times the noise of distant guns provoked false alarms, and set pulses beating madly but it was not until well after midnight that the sound of a train was heard. It could not be seen but the chug chug and the rumble and rattle were unmistakable. Rifle bolts clicked and the machine gunners shifted their bodies to more comfortable firing positions.

The noise slowly increased as the train rumbled along the stretch of straight lines. The men in the ambush grew tense, their eyes staring transfixed up the line, their fingers lightly compressing triggers with the sure touch that comes from experience. On came the train, unsuspecting, to certain disaster four hundred yards away, its outline clear; two hundred yards with a billow of smoke, then less than fifty yards, majestic in the pale light, roaring in defiance.

The crash shook the onlookers to the very marrow of their bones as the engine ran on and off the track, bucked like a wild horse and hissed like a snake. Wheels ploughed up the sleepers; coal flew in all directions as the engine and its two wagons thundered and rattled to a grinding bumpy halt seventy yards ahead. Steam and smoke rose in a low dense cloud, hiding the engine and its occupants. The noise slowly subsided and the men of D Company recovered from their shock. A Very light hissed skyward and burst, lighting up the black engine, still upright, gaunt and still. A shot rang out from the engine cabin. It acted as a signal and started a hail of bullets from the nearest machine gun.

Four Jap bodies were found but little else except the loads of cut timber in the wagons and the men wondered why such a risk should be incurred by the Jap merely to move planks. Brian Rogers was both puzzled and disappointed for the four Japs could have been four hundred, and their fate the same. It was the last train from Mandalay, however.

It was 22 March and the day proved to be frustrating, anxious and sad with only losses to show and no gains. The battalion moved out at 0730 hours under heavy Jap shelling and behind the 1/3 Gurkha Rifles, who were going to attack. By midday, Jap and Gurkha were locked together and neither could move forward or backward. A mortar regiment came tearing along the road and set their weapons up in a field. In a few minutes bombs were whistling in a steady stream towards the enemy. Shells screamed overhead from 25 pounders, and crumped on the village in rapid succession. In reply, a Jap 75mm gun spat three times viciously down the road, shattering the nerves but doing no real damage. Vic established the H.Q. in the curve of a large dry ditch, and reclining on the soft bank, waited and watched.

The Mortars changed tactics, and sent a score of smoke bombs shooting up in a steep arc to fall on the wooden houses, but the hoped for fires did not start. 'Arson Incorporated' was the adopted name for this new technique of burning out the Jap, and which was only employed when the situation was desperate.

Suddenly, the Jap 75mm gun sent six vicious little shells along the road in rapid succession, and everybody disappeared into the ditch, hating that little gun. The first thing the receiving end knew about it was the sharp explosion of the actual shell. Its killing area was small but the sudden explosions were unnerving.

The tedium of the morning was relieved by orders to move forward and to send a platoon of Sikhs around the back of the village with a troop of tanks. The Gurkhas, who were preparing to storm the village, needed some close support and an ambush for the Japs who, it was expected, would run east away into the arms of the Sikhs.

The battle suddenly flared up. Half a dozen Hurricanes circled above and one after the other they dived and bombed. Hundreds of shells were sent whistling and crashing into the village and then, as the Gurkhas started to move, the mortars dropped bomb after bomb twenty or thirty yards ahead of the forward troops, but all to no avail and within a couple of hours the 6th Punjabis were covering the withdrawal of the Gurkhas, who filed past in the ditches, silent and without their customary good humour.

Dick Smedley was ordered to return to base and the battalion prepared to move, but there was a hold up; the poor platoon of A Company was being attacked and had great difficulty in extricating itself and the tanks, sustaining two killed and nine wounded in the process. The biter had been bitten and the boy who went to do a man's job badly mauled.

Vic walked alongside the C.O. as the battalion, carrying their wounded, made their way back to Meiktila, and for some time neither spoke, each deep in thought.

'Not a good day, sir,' Vic ventured at last.

'Good God, no Vic,' said Colonel Smedley a little sharply.

'It seems to me that brigade made a mistake in sending one platoon around the back. We could all have gone or at least two full companies and given the Jap a real crack,' Vic said.

'You are probably right, but the Jap was tougher than the Gurkhas expected. There's another show tomorrow.'

For the first time during the past three weeks the battalion was complete in one place. At once preparations for the next day's big attack started. The C.O. went to Brigade H.Q. for orders, and returned within half an hour.

'This is it,' he said to Vic. 'Tomorrow we are mounting a set piece attack against the Jap on the high ground by the lake. Ask the officers to come for briefing in ten minutes. Then we will get down to the details.'

On paper, the air and artillery support for the attack seemed more than adequate and included pattern bombing by Mitchell bombers, dive bombers, heavy and continuous shelling by all available guns in addition to the full support of the Mortar Regiment.

It was obvious during the evening meal that the significance of the proposed attack had not been fully appreciated by all concerned, but two or three company commanders, having studied the maps of the area, were worried, particularly with regard to the open ground which lay between the starting point and the Jap positions, which were known to be heavily fortified.

The stretch of open ground overlooked by the enemy, was some seven hundred yards across, and obviously would be swept by small arms fire unless the bombardment was one hundred percent effective. A heavy smoke barrage had been arranged to hide the troop's movements over the final one hundred yards and on paper it appeared that the supporting fire power was more than sufficient.

At the scheduled time of 0730 hours, the battalion set off, deployed in single file with one jeep carrying the wireless, moving at marching pace in the centre. For a mile, the route was almost due south into the heart of battered Meiktila where, in reasonably good cover, the pace quickened and the direction changed.

Through rows of wooden shacks and houses, past a pagoda here and there, the files of men moved steadily. For a mile and a half the march continued to the west and the sun shone warmly on the backs of the men who with rifles slung over their shoulders moved almost in a jaunty manner. Presently, the advanced elements turned north toward the assembly area, which lay behind the top of a hill and stretched across the front for some thousand yards. The pace slackened and the men picked their route with greater caution up the gentle slope, using the cover of a building which stood empty, gaunt and neglected. Vic wondered as he walked past where the owners had gone, and whether they were pro or anti Jap.

A few yards from the top of the hill the scouts halted behind a thick wall and bounding the north edge of a most convenient metalled road, which joined a main road about six hundred yards farther on. Near the road junction and almost on the summit of the hill a beautiful stately pagoda rose, blue and white in the morning sun, its spire high above the surrounding trees. The weather was pleasant, the sun not yet too strong and hot. The battalion took up its battle positions and waited.

Away to the right, the Gurkhas were in position, their left flank troops in contact with the 6th Punjabis east flank, and no doubt exchanging greetings and talking about everything except the job in hand. The enemy were dug in seven hundred yards away. Vic set up his H.Q. behind the wall, and during the next twenty minutes, wireless sets were checked and rechecked. Vic received a report from D Company who were carrying out a feint attack eight hundred yards to the west, that all was well.

The minutes passed slowly and the waiting became oppressive. The men began to fidget uneasily, adjusting their equipment and conjecturing in whispers.

The atmosphere was tense and electric. The jeeps which had brought the generals were tucked away in cover behind the hill. Then came the drone of approaching aircraft and about thirty Mitchell bombers came in sight, flying at about two thousand feet, their engines making speech impossible as they flew overhead and wheeled. In impressive formation they reached the Jap position. All eyes were riveted, watching for the bombs which tumbled out like peas from the pod and exploded with somewhat disappointing bangs amongst the trees. A squadron of snub-nosed single engine planes appeared without warning, broke formation, and dived one after the other firing cannons. Behind them a dozen Hurricanes zoomed over the target, dropped their bombs, circled, strafed the enemy positions with cannon fire and disappeared. Shells began to whistle overhead, crashing it seemed with more effect than the bombs, and heartening the soldiers who were now waiting for the signal to advance.

Hands on watches crept around to the appointed hour, and then the leading men stood up, clambered over the wall and moved forward at a fast walking pace.

The continuous stream of artillery and mortar shells and bombs filled the air with a deafening thunder. Down the slope from out of the shadow of the trees and into the flat open country the soldiers moved; rifles ready, with bullets up the spout. One hundred yards . . . two hundred yards . . . three hundred yards, and the half distance mark was passed. No shots were fired. Five paces between each man the companies moved forward, steady and resolute. Through the tall grass and patchy scrub the men advanced, keeping perfect formation, weapons at the ready, eyes searching the ground ahead and the dark shadows of the trees in which the enemy wait, barely three hundred and fifty yards away.

From out of the trees at any moment there would come the vicious, killing machine gun fire. The advance does not slacken. Suddenly, Vic, earphones fixed, walking behind the wireless carrier like a dog on a lead, received the order 'Withdraw at once!'

Before he can answer a woman's voice loud and foreign

comes on the air gabbling like a gaggle of geese. The wave-length is jammed. He cannot speak to the leading companies who are still moving forward. He tries to interrupt the woman but she continues without pause and his voice was drowned by her incoherent chatter.

The significance of the withdrawal order flashed through his mind; something must have gone wrong. The attack must be stopped. The leading troops are almost in the open country, barely three hundred yards from the enemy positions. They must withdraw at once. But there was no wireless contact.

Angry and anxious he rips off the earphones. He must stop the attack. B and C are almost there. They will be slaughtered. The thoughts flashed through his mind. He raises his hand bellowing 'Halt!' at the top of his voice. The men around stop and lie down. 'Withdraw' Vic shouts.

'Shamroz, run like hell to Stanley Sahib, and tell him to withdraw at once. I'll go to B Company. Quick!' he shouts.

Vic, head down, runs the one hundred and fifty yards as fast as he can across the open ground, swerving only to avoid an advancing soldier who stares in amazement.

Almost breathless, he calls John, 'For Christ's sake, John, withdraw, withdraw!' Major Smythe does not question or even pause to enquire the reason. With the Japs so near there is no time to argue, and he immediately orders his men to withdraw at the double.

Within a few minutes, both companies were back in the assembly area, and Vic, whitefaced and shaken listens in silence while Robin London explains the reason for the sudden change in plan. The General, who had watched the air strike, had decided that it had been inadequate for a frontal assault, and had order the attack to be postponed.

'Surely there was time to send us a message earlier,' Vic protested.

The Japs, who had seen the operation were as mystified as the British but quickly recovered and began shelling. Heavy salvos crashed one after the other into the assembly area, and six men were wounded before a pause enabled the soldiers to get under cover.

Nothing happened until the late afternoon. Until then the position was shelled continuously with great skill. Not, apparently, having a great deal of ammunition, the Jap used it carefully, but with devastating effect. A dozen shells exploded, followed by a pause of five or ten minutes, during which nerves and pulses returned to near normal. Then two or three single shells at irregular intervals would crash among the men, setting the butterflies in stomachs fluttering and hands and legs atremble.

Another pause, perhaps a long one, during which everyone recovered and began to think that the shelling had really ended.

Then a dozen shells would crash almost simultaneously among the trees, which bore the scars of many direct hits. Irregular shelling with irregular pauses for hours on end is demoralising and it was not until the troops had managed to scratch a hole in the granite-like ground that the worst effects of the shelling were diminished.

Vic made frequent radio calls to Brigade H.Q. and received orders to withdraw D Company who were protecting the left flank and now in position among the trees on the west side of the main road. It was obvious that their withdrawal was going to be difficult, for the Japs were constantly shelling targets in their rear, so it was decided that Vic should act as their guide. He and Shamroz waited for a lull in the shelling and started to move westwards using the low wall as best they could. They crouched low as they moved, bent double, by the soldiers sheltering behind the wall.

Warned by a terrifying screech, Vic and Shamroz suddenly flung themselves against the wall and waited with bated breath for the shells to burst with a deafening crash. Then, a little more shaken, and dusty, they hurry on towards the road, their progress being halted again and again. One shell hits the stout wall, bits of stone and mortar fly in all directions, and the earth and wall against which they are pressed, shudders and trembles. Whilst the wall stands upright, thick and strong, and shell-proof, they are safe. Not until they came to the end of it and a patch of exposed ground beyond, do the two men feel afraid.

They dash toward cover behind the pagoda, get caught in a salvo of shells, spot a wooden hut and fall inside bursting the door catch with their momentum. They lie on the floor panting, trembling and scared. A quiet voice says, 'Here, drink this, it will do you good.' Vic looks up into the eyes of a kindly bespectacled face, pale beneath its tan and blinks as he recognised where he is. With as much dignity as he could muster, he scrambles to his feet. 'You're an angel in disguise,' he says, takes a gulp of brandy and passed the glass to Shamroz.

'I must apologise for bursting into your medical aid post,' Vic says breathlessly.

'Oh, that's all right,' replies the Indian doctor. 'You were just in time. I'm waiting for the ambulance to get these two back,' indicating the two sepoys lying on stretchers, 'and then I'm going to find a safer hole.'

They shake hands as if they had known each other for years, naturally and without demonstration, and part.

It is quiet outside as Vic and Shamroz walk across the road into the wooded slopes towards D Company who can be seen about a furlong ahead. Three wounded are being carried, and the speed of the withdrawal is being regulated by that of the stretcher bearers, but within twenty minutes the battalion is assembled and ready to move. Several more casualties have occurred from the last salvoes, which prove to be the Japs' final effort for the time being.

When the C.O. returns with orders to move there is a rapid forming up, all glad to be leaving such a hot spot. The battalion wended its way widely dispersed in single file to its nw home situated a mile or so south in the shelter of woods which grew beside the lake. Through the broken down, battered and derelict houses the men moved quickly and in silence until the leading sections turned down a track into the cool shadows of the trees.

Then, just as everybody felt secure and safely hidden, the Jap struck. No-one heard the warning scream of the shells for none went overhead. Instead they landed amidst the standing troops who, in momentary panic dived for cover. Twenty to thirty shells suddenly exploded ripping through the trees, and creating a violent storm of dust, bits of earth and red hot metal splinters.

The noise subsided into a deathly silence. No-one moved. A branch of a tree cracked; men got closer to cover and then relaxed feeling stupid as the branch quivered, snapped and tumbled down. A wounded soldier cried out, provoking the battalion into action. The incident which had lasted only two or three minutes left three bodies for burial, and eight badly wounded. The casualties were lighter than expected, and Vic standing beside the C.O. said, 'Thank God we had not closed up, and for the soft ground. We might have lost half the battalion.'

The day had been bad, frustrating and fruitless. Sixteen men had been wounded, three killed, not a round had been fired at the Jap, and it was a depressed and puzzled battalion that dug in by the edge of the lake, and buried its dead.

Shells continued to fall in ones or twos for an hour, but fell harmlessly into the lake. Vic's dug-out had been cut out from the bank of the lake and he sat in it watching the shells fall in the water. He felt shaken, hungry, and afraid. Inside his dug-out he was safe but the food was a hundred yards away across an open space.

Presently, he plucked up his courage and walked swiftly to the improvised mess, where in the failing light two or three officers sat in silence, eating stew. It was a welcome meal, and washed down with strong tea, put new life into Vic, but he returned to his hole as soon as it was decently possible.

The shells were getting fewer and still two hundred yards off target. Soon they stopped altogether and Vic breathed a sigh of relief, and as he prepared for bed he paused to admire the sun, red, resplendent, and half-hidden behind the lake. He watched in deep thought as the water became golden, then grey and dark until only its white horses could be seen as they lapped the shore. He sat still, motionless, reflecting on the events of the day.

'A few more days like this,' he thought, 'and we shan't last long. There can't be any worse days, and tomorrow will be better. After all, we only need a successful attack and tails will be up again.' He grimaced as he recalled the voice probably of a Burmese which had jammed their wave-length and who was obviously spotting for the Japs. He believed she had seen them turn off the road into the wood, and brought down the shells. She must be nearby in a tall building. Tomorrow she would be found. Vic dismissed her from his mind and crawled into his hole.

For the next few days the lakeside camp became the base from which intense patrolling was carried out with moderate success. It was obvious that another full scale attack would be needed to destroy the enemy who were now delaying the advance to Rangoon, and it came as no surprise when orders were received on 27 March to attack.

At 0200 hours when the night was very dark, Vic struggled into his equipment, and sluiced his face with cold water. His mug of strong tea was welcome and he sipped it appreciatively, thinking of the task ahead. He felt a sense of relief, a spirit of exultation, for today he thought, we will smash the Meiktila Jap and open the road to Rangoon.

A few hours later he lay in the undergrowth of the assembly area, waiting again for the air strike and artillery bombardment. This time there was no excitement, no impressive spectacle, and the planes, although more numerous, did not attract much attention, and after they had dropped their bombs and zoomed away, the advance commenced.

From overhead, the sun bore down fiercely as the leading troops picked their way through the prickly scrub with weapons loaded and bayonets fixed. Four hundred yards were covered without incident, while on the left a stream of shells poured into the heart of the enemy position, and Hurricanes strafed enemy targets with cannon and machine guns. Major Douglas, the leading company commander, reported no enemy in sight, and with increasing confidence the troops approached the centre of the fortified position, now only four hundred yards away.

Suddenly, a hundred rifles cracked almost simultaneously. Machine guns started chattering, and grenades exploded adding their deep boom to the already deafening noise. Twenty yards ahead every bush became alive and from them came a stream of fire, deadly in its accuracy, deathly in effect. The leading unit went to ground to return bullet for bullet. The Japs had come out to fight but their individual holes in the centre of each bush could not be seen even at a few yards range; only the brief glint of a barrel and the faint puffs of smoke gave away their positions. Caught at a disadvantage without good cover, C Company quickly lost a score of men in killed and wounded. They fought back, and soon levelled the score.

Indians and Japs died alike in the hot midday sun, their bodies slumped grotesquely behind bushes, in the small deep holes and in the open. Stretcher bearers in pairs, panting and sweating from their exertions in the heat, crawled forward from cover to cover pulling and pushing their stretchers until, gasping, with a final heave, they collected a half-conscious sepoy and started on the arduous return journey to safety.

For three and a half hours the battle raged without pause, and the Japs were forced back a hundred yards. Then B Company attempted a leap-frog action through the ground held by C

Company. The Japs waited and watched, their eyes just clear of the ground, and when the Punjabis were within thirty yards, they opened fire. With bayonets fixed and rifles blazing from the hip, B Company went on, gaining the thirty yards before being stopped in their tracks by intense fire which swept the area from the flanks and front.

Major Douglas was on his feet exhorting his men to move to better positions so that more help could be given to B Company. He was seen by a Jap marksman and killed instantly. Blow after blow fell upon the battalion as they struggled to advance against a fanatical enemy who died rather than withdraw, and against the sun which bore down, scorching the men until they became dizzy with fatigue, and their weapons too hot to touch.

That night, the divisional commander threw a ring of men, guns and tanks around the Jap, whose west flank was bounded by the lake, and the many units involved linked up with each other to prevent the enemy's escape, It was thought that they would attempt to break out under cover of darkness, so strong patrols went forward to observe and ambush.

Sleep was impossible as men rested uneasily with rifles loaded. Their clothing, soaked with sweat, cold and clammy, clung tight to their bodies. They tried to ignore the mosquitoes that buzzed and dived like miniature Hurricanes. An uneasy hush came with the darkness, and the soldiers lying in their shallow trenches waited, eyes straining, searching the night for signs of movement, but none came. No shot was fired, and none of the booby traps which had been placed between the bushes in front of the position were detonated.

The night was very long. With the anxious dawn, orders came to remain static and with the information that other units were advancing toward the Jap from the south. When at last orders were received to resume the attack, the battalion cautiously worked through the prickly scrub toward the new objective. It was occupied without opposition. The ring of steel had closed in on the enemy position, but the Jap had gone, leaving only two or three damaged guns and half a dozen corpses. It was uncanny. Yesterday the area was full of Japs, perhaps a thousand or more, with machine guns, at least two dozen pieces of artillery, ammunition, supplies, and many wounded. Yet today there was nothing.

Apart from the west boundary where the lake, wide and deep,

prevented escape, all the areas to the north, east and south had been thick with Allied troops, cleverly disposed, and alert; and yet without a bush being disturbed or a shot fired, the Japs had moved out unhampered and undamaged.

The incredibility of the situation overwhelmed and sank without trace the feeling of frustration and of being cheated, which in other circumstances would have aroused deep anger.

A war correspondent by the name of Clive Graham arrived, causing a minor sensation, for he was one of the first of the very few who covered the Eastern Front and it seemed to Vic, who talked to him and his escort, a Sikh P.R.O., rather unfortunate that his visit should have coincided with the escape of the Jap, which was apparently of little news value.

8

SOUTH TO RANGOON

With the immediate area of Meiktila completely clear of enemy, the 17th Indian Division turn enquiring eyes toward Rangoon three hundred and forty miles to the south. Thazi, twelve miles due east, is still Jap occupied. Between Meiktila and Mandalay, in the north, there is a large enemy force consisting of the six enemy divisions which have been moved to defend the old capital. In the west, at Chauk and at Yenanyaung oilfields, there are large concentrations of Japanese. The road south to Rangoon is held in force at several places and particularly at Pyawbwe, where the withdrawing enemy are concentrating.

On 31 March the battalion moved toward Thazi, a small town twelve miles to the east. A patrol soon made contact with a much larger enemy force, who were particularly aggressive, and who appeared intent on attack, then they hesitated and made off in the direction of Thazi.

Thazi lay in low ground about one thousand yards away, and from a tree top could be seen quite clearly. Preparations were soon made for artillery and air bombardment, and within an hour the air seemed full of Hurricanes and light bombers who circled waiting for instructions from the ground.

Harry, a flight lieutenant of the Royal Canadian Air Force, who had been attached to the brigade for some time was the ground-to-air wireless link using a V.H.F. set which was fitted most efficiently in a jeep trailer. Vic climbed a tree, seated himself on a branch in reasonable comfort, and with binoculars selected targets, shouting down their position to Harry, who relayed to the aircraft and to the artillery forward observation officer who passed the details to the gun positions.

Several Jap positions received direct hits, and one, situated near a pagoda about four hundred yards south of Thazi was shelled, bombed and strafed with cannon and machine guns. Vic saw a lot of movement in its vicinity, and fresh earth of a sizeable area which seemed to indicate a recently dug position. The pagoda formed an excellent aiming mark, the system of communication from ground to air worked well and a dozen Hurricanes dive-bombed the target with great accuracy. The 25-pounders took over, dead on target, and a great weight of shells pounded the area till it seemed that not even an insect could live within fifty yards of the pagoda.

With his binoculars, Vic watched and waited for signs of life or death as the clouds of dust disappeared. He saw the target area emerge, studded with craters. Minutes passed and nothing happened. Then from the north edge of the fresh earth, six ant-like figures seemed to crawl out from underneath a crater. They stood up, formed single file, paused for a second or so, casually brushed the dust off their clothes, and moved off.

Their position during the bombardment received several direct hits and many near misses, but judging from their casual manner, they might well have been coming out of a barber's shop. Vic gazed transfixed, unable to believe his eyes, which followed the little figures until they were swallowed up in the dark background, and then uttering, 'Well, I'll be damned!' loudly to himself, swung down from the tree and saw a jeep turning in the road.

In it sat General 'Punch' Cowan, the divisional commander, and General Demoline, the C.R.A. who expertly manoeuvred the little vehicle, which shot away up the road like a racing car at Brooklands. Harry was grinning.

'I tried to tell you they were here, but for the last ten minutes you sat up there squinting through your binoculars in a world of your own. Anyway, they seemed pleased that we were on target.'

'They didn't see the ones who got away,' replied Vic, and described the incident of the six Japs.

'There must be ten feet of earth at least on top of that dug-out, supported with timber, and with a blast proof entrance,' Harry remarked. 'The Japs certainly know how to build a defensive position.'

Harry had been preparing to move off, and sat ready at the wheel. 'This isn't my idea of spending a Saturday afternoon,' he said in his light Canadian accent, 'but I can think of more unpleasant ways, and no doubt we'll be seeing each other again in more convivial circumstances.'

John Smythe, commanding the large standing patrol on the other side of Thazi came through on the radio on Sunday morning, reporting a lot of enemy activity in the area around Thazi. An hour later Brian Rogers jubilantly reported a successful ambush in which a complete patrol of twenty Japs were killed within a mile of the battalion position.

'What happened?' enquired Vic.

'It was a piece of cake,' he said, 'we saw them a mile away. They were hurrying toward Thazi and we waited in a copse until they were in our trap. In two minutes it was all over. We are now coming in for breakfast.'

'Congratulations, I'll put the kettle on,' replied Vic, and rang off.

An hour later when the sun was becoming very hot, the battalion turned south and set off to attack a small village, one and a half miles south-west of Thazi. Over the hard and uneven ground the men moved rapidly, glad to be going southwards at last towards Rangoon, their final target.

Without a halt the village was entered, searched and found empty. A larger village, Zidaw, which lay a mile further south was next on the list, and within an hour they were under light shell fire. The patrolling parties sustained several casualties from 75mm guns in Zidaw which was then heavily bombarded and dive-bombed. It was too late for an attack and a cordon of patrols were placed around the village to observe and ambush. An excited platoon commander came through on the wirless to report that thirty or forty Japs were assembled sitting on their bottoms having their evening meal.

'Keep watching from two hundred yards range and we'll put down some artillery,' Vic replied.

Tom Clarke, the artillery officer, was only too keen to oblige, murmuring, 'How very careless of them. We must teach them a lesson. I think perhaps two shells each will do the trick.'

The C.O. who had joined the little group of officers and wireless operators, agreed at once, and eighty shells hurtled towards the eating Japs. The patrol leader came through on the wireless reporting about twelve killed and fifteen or sixteen wounded.

During the night the Japs were either aggressive or just trigger happy, for they started firing rather indiscriminately in the direction of our patrols, who immediately brought down artillery fire which eventually discouraged the enemy, permitting both sides, except for patrols and sentries, to get a few hours sleep.

Away to the north east of Thazi, John Smythe was having a sleepless night. Shots were being fired into his position at irregular intervals, and in the pale moonlight his men frequently saw Japs who appeared to be trying to discover his strength. Tempted as they were by the appearance of good targets, the Punjabis refrained from returning the fire, thereby earning themselves a good mark for fire discipline, and certainly saving some of their lives. When dawn came and the sun peeped over the hills, the expected attack did not materialise. Instead, the enemy hesitated, obviously unsure of themselves, and took up positions on all sides of the area. John received permission to withdraw at his own discretion which made him feel much more comfortable. His role had been achieved; he had given the impression to the enemy that Thazi was going to be attacked, whereas, in fact, the general had no such intention and was content to allow the Japs the freedom of the town while his division pushed on to Rangoon. The more Japs who stayed in Thazi, the fewer the division would meet on their way to the capital. A day had been gained, and another would pass before the Japs realised that they had been outwitted and left behind.

John made his plan to withdraw for now there was no real point in remaining outnumbered by ten to one without mortar or artillery support. He had been without sleep for almost forty eight hours; his men were tired and hungry and there were more than a thousand Japanese in the vicinity. The rest of the battalion were moving further away and there was no likelihood of any reinforcements being sent to help.

Moving in twos and threes his men crept carefully through the Jap positions, while the rear party drew the enemy attention and fire. Within two hours, the operation was completed without casualties, and once out of range, the party moved swiftly to join the battalion.

In the command post, Vic had been receiving half hourly reports from B Company and was now receiving them from C

Company, who were trying to occupy a dry river bed a quarter of a mile or so north of Zidaw.

Mike Boon, A Company commander, was keeping himself informed of the situation, his long form stretched almost lazily on the hard ground, and with head cupped in hands he faced the bevy of wireless sets. He and his company had been in almost constant action for the past month. Both had displayed great skill and guts, and now, as he waited to lead the Sikhs in another attack, Mike's manner was alert and attentive, but quite composed.

His eyes wandered to the Mortar Regiment as they crouched around their upturned drainpipes, making final adjustments to range and direction, and then he stood up, smoothing his blond hair with an instinctive casual gesture of the right hand, and strode off with long purposeful strides to his company who were resting under cover to the left.

Everything now was ready except for the two troops of tanks, and the squadron of armoured cars, now overdue. Vic began to get anxious and wirlessed Brigade H.Q. who replied that the cars and tanks were on their way. It was too late to stop the air strike for Hurricanes and Thunderbolts were overhead and their time over the target was limited by their fuel carrying capacity. It was decided that the attack should start without the tank and armoured car support. The planes zoomed down in almost vertical dives with guns belching and cannons blasting the enemy positions. Guns from a mile or so to the rear sent a stream of 25 pounder shells whistling overhead to crash on the village. The nearby four and three inch Mortars popped into action to give close support to the now advancing troops.

For ten minutes the inferno raged, bombs, guns, cannons, shells and mortars whined, roared, and crashed. The infantry had a long way to go, almost a quarter of a mile across wide open country, and when the bombardment ceased, they were alone and without supporting fire. The tanks and cars were still missing.

Quick as lightening the Japs opened fire with gun and small arms and within seconds ten of the attacking troops lay dead or wounded. The attack was halted, mortars fired smoke instead of high explosives, and under its choking, blinding cover A and C Companies scrambled hurriedly back to the safety of the river bed. The bombardment had failed and the attack had cost casualties without gain, but several hours of light remained and could not be wasted.

The air hummed with orders from brigade to battalion, from battalion to the companies, to the guns, to the air force, to the mortars, and by this time to the tanks and armoured cars, who had just arrived. They had been unavoidably delayed and could not be blamed for the loss of life.

The wireless hummed again. Brigade wanted to know the time of the next attack, and Vic, who took the message muttered, 'Why the devil can't they wait instead of interrupting?'

Tons of high explosive pounded the village as the infantry advanced a second time. Tanks and cars in hull-down position swept the village with an intense storm of machine gun fire, and while the Japs kept their heads down, A and C Companies attacked and entered Zidaw.

The battle went well and good progress was being made when, from the left where the tanks and cars were positioned, came heavy and accurate machine gunfire directed at the Sikhs. Instantly tempers flared. A Company suffered badly, and Mike Boon who was in constant wireless contact with battalion H.Q. shouted, 'For heavens sake stop those bloody fools.'

But the damage had been done, men had died and been wounded, and those who escaped were bitter, angry, and without confidence in the tank support.

Vic, angry and anxious swore violently at the tank squadron commander, and was immediately sorry. The tanks ceased fire and the attack went on. House after house was charged and its defenders killed in hand to hand combat. Grenades rolled into the deep dug-outs, their explosions reverberating through the linking tunnels.

Many Japs pressed grenades to their stomachs and released the pins, leaving ghastly sights of bloody entrails, shattered hands and arms. Others withdrew to escape the fury of the Sikhs who now were intent only on revenge, and fighting with rifle and bayonet without fear, pity, or remorse. But the Jap, tough and courageous as ever, concentrated on the southern tip of the village and held out until the darkness saved them. They had sent three vehicles dashing southwards just before dusk; our tanks, which had moved south, used their six pounders, but the trucks careered madly along the rough track, with clouds of dust in their wake, forged on and escaped. The Jap army was far from defeated.

The light had begun to fade when back across the battlefield came the Sikhs and Jats. They came in silence and no word was spoken as they moved into the darkness of the trees. They came slowly with heavy legs and hearts, and Vic, standing motionless on the edge of the copse felt their grief and sorrow. Twenty men had been killed, and twenty-five wounded, some very badly, and those who lived were exhausted in both body and spirit; close friends had been parted and lost for ever. The fire of the fight had gone out of the survivors and now they felt only the sadness of death. As the last section disappeared into the trees, Vic turned and followed them.

From the time of the first attack, the M.O., Captain Deitra and his staff had worked under terrible conditions and with inadequate equipment. Under the fierce Burma sun, he and his stretcher bearers had gone out, sometimes ahead of the fighting soldiers, to bring in the wounded, who lay helpless, sometimes dying, and always with parched throats. Four members of the American Field Service, who had attached themselves to the battalion, drove their jeep ambulances as far as the dry river bed, and went forward on foot again and again in complete disregard of their own safety. They were under no obligation to serve in such a manner nor were they asked, but their sense of duty was high and fine, and their conduct during the day drew sincere and spontaneous praise from everybody.

Evacuation of the casualties was being carried out against time as it was not safe to send ambulances back to Meiktila during darkness, for the road was not held. When the light failed completely about a dozen wounded remained in the battalion area, and two, with bad stomach wounds were in a serious condition. The doctor was worried and went to see the adjutant.

'These two men ought to be operated on tonight Vic, otherwise they will die. The Americans have volunteered to take them back to Meiktila but I'm not very happy about letting them go. They might easily get ambushed and lose their lives too.'

Vic did not reply for a moment and then said, 'Get the wounded ready Doc, I'll provide an escort, then we'll both have a chat with the Americans.'

Colonel Smedley gave his approval, and Vic detailed an

N.C.O. and three Sepoys, armed with two light machine guns and two tommy guns, to be ready in ten minutes, then hurried off to see the Americans. They were quite willing to take a chance on getting through; in fact, the alternative course, which would permit them to remain in relative safety for the night whilst the two wounded died, had not occurred to them.

'It's considerate of the Doc,' the senior one said, 'but we will take the wounded back and be pleased to do it. Its the least we can do to help.'

Vic's heart went out to the unassuming softly spoken Americans who had travelled thousands of miles from their homes to serve strange soldiers in a strange and unfriendly country.

The three men stumbled through the darkness to where the escort sat waiting. Vic explained that Japs might be met on the road, adding, 'Take the screens off the headlights, and when you are about a quarter of a mile from here, the first jeep will drive with all lights until you are within a quarter of a mile of brigade, when all lights must go out except the side ones. I'll warn brigade.'

'If you meet Japs, the headlights will cause them to hesitate. Don't stop, but increase speed; they won't be able to aim against the lights and if you press on, you will get through. If you see Japs on the road, the L.M.Gs in the first jeep will open fire but don't stop unless it's absolutely impossible to proceed. If this should happen, the rear jeep will switch on its lights and its two gunners will open fire and endeavour to free the first jeep.'

Vic wished them good luck and watched the jeeps picking their way between trees and ditches. He saw the headlights stab the darkness and then fade away in the distance.

He made his way through the trees, which loomed up in front of him with a frightening suddenness, and in between the foxholes where men rested, still and silent, until he made out the faint outline of a Sikh, guarding the medical post. Vic opened the door and pulled aside the thick blanket which hung on the inside.

In the far corner two small electric bulbs dangled from the timber rafters. A kettle on the primus stove hissed and the odour of paraffin mingled with the smell of antiseptic. A bench had been fixed up under the lights and on it lay a Sikh clothed only in a blanket from which one leg protruded. The Doc was probing the leg with a silvery instrument.

Vic stood still in the shadow, and waited watching as the doctor finished his probing, and cleaned the two jagged holes in the man's calf. The patient's beard glistened with perspiration, his eyes followed the doctor's hands as if fascinated. He was quiet and motionless as a statue. A few minutes passed before the doctor straightened.

'There you are my friend, you will be all right in a few days,' adding to an orderly, 'bandage him up, and I'll see him in the morning. See that he gets his food and some rum.' To Vic, he said, 'I think that's the lot. My goodness what a day!' He washed his hands carefully, then asked, 'Are we getting any reinforcements?'

'There are some on the way, but its a long way from India. Come and have a drink, you look all in,' said Vic.

'I don't want many more days like today. I've had over forty casualties.' His gravelly voice was hoarse.

'Are they very bad?' enquired Vic.

'There's about half a dozen with shell wounds, who won't be back for months, seven with bad stomach wounds who won't be back at all, but the rest are mainly flesh wounds like the Sikh you saw. It's a good job the Jap bullets are only .026, but there are a number of wounded who were hit with .303 bullets from our tanks.'

Under the tarpaulin which, pegged down on one side from the side of a truck, formed the mess, the C.O. sat on his tiny canvas chair drinking coffee.

'Come on you two,' the colonel said, 'you both look dead beat.'

The orderly handed over two glasses containing good pegs of whisky, and then disappeared into the shadows and returned with two plates of stew. The two men ate in silence until the C.O. broke into the thoughts of his two officers.

'I'm glad that the wounded got through all right. I received a message a few minutes before you came in.'

Soon after, he announced, 'I'll turn in. Let me know if anything happens during the night. Good night.'

The C.O. rose, folded his chair and walked off into the night.

'The colonel is looking tired,' the doctor said.

'Yes, he has had a bloody day. We have lost a lot of good men. I think its time we got a few hours rest too. We start again at dawn. Between now and then, anything can happen.'

The two men bade each other good night and went their separate ways.

Just after dawn, Zidaw was occupied without resistance and another village was available for reoccupation by the Burmese. Sixty three Japanese corpses were found.

When the dead had been buried, all ranks relaxed. Officers dawdled over innumerable cups of coffee, reading their personal mail, and waiting for the relief battalion. There was an air of expectancy, and a feeling of cheerful optimism. The morning was bright and fresh and the melancholy caused by heavy casualties had disappeared, and when a battalion of the Dogra Regiment of 19 Division literally burst upon the scene, they received a very friendly welcome. Their leading troops swept through the cluster of huts in a business-like manner before they stopped and fraternised in a way that troops in such circumstances love so much.

The meeting of the two battalions ended the first phase in the campaign. 19th Indian Division who, with 2nd British Division, had captured Mandalay, had joined up with 17th Indian Division conquerors of Meiktila. Now the 14th Army could march on to Rangoon.

9

THE RACE IS ON

That night there was a heavy storm, the first rain for months, and the camp was flooded, but the sun came out with the dawn as the battalion moved off. For the first time the direction of their advance was toward Rangoon. Across rough uneven paddy fields, over ranges of small hills, through rivers and villages, everybody hunted the Jap.

As one force, but more often split into several, and fighting in three or four different places at the same time, the 6th Punjabis pushed on with all speed. One bright morning, the Sikhs routed an enemy force in double quick time. They were moving down a long slight incline when the scouts, two hundred yards ahead, disturbed a party of twenty five Japs who made off towards the east. At once the Sikhs charged across country in full cry like a pack of hounds. In ten minutes, the Japs were dead, and the advance was resumed with a sepoy carrying a magnificent Japanese ceremonial sword. For sheer speed in attack this was indeed a record.

Split into three and sometimes four parties, the battalion headed south at a cracking pace, over miles of flat country; up and down the sides of stony hills, along dry river beds and through villages men hurried, panting and sweating under the intense heat of the Burma sun. Another party of Japs hiding in the thick scrub, were winkled out with bayonets. The village of Kyattiunkala was suddenly bombarded by every available plane and gun, prior to a vicious battalion assault which yielded a score of enemy dead and five 75mm guns.

One night, the resting place was a pleasant clean Burmese village with stout timber houses, and a good supply of crystal clear cool water. Only one Burmese remained in it. He knelt in the open space in the centre of the village, his hands were tied behind his back, his head was bruised and battered. He was very old and very thin. He had been beaten to death. His burial was quick and his body was lowered into the warm earth in silence. Another friend had gone, savaged to death without reason, save that of remaining in his village.

Preparations were made to attack another village which was obviously strongly occupied. A lot of movement could be seen and what appeared to be a dozen vehicles. Vic advised brigade of the intention to attack. An artillery plan was made and the battalion advanced, but when the forward troops were within four hundred yards of the village, it became apparent that the village was occupied by Brigade H.Q. itself, who, quite unaware of the true position and thus indifferent to their rapidly approaching fate, were making tea and, no doubt, congratulating themselves on finding such a pleasant village in which to pass the night! Since the battalion were the advance guard of the brigade, reporting its position at regular intervals, and indeed had advised brigade of the proposed attack, it was obvious that the map reading of either the battalion or the brigade had been wrong. Brigade H.Q. had never before led an advance.

When it was confirmed that it was brigade who were at fault, the 6th Punjabis moved through the village enquiring as they passed whether the brigade would care to borrow a guide, and pressed on to Mixiywathit, a large village a mile or so to the south. No Japs were found immediately but a party of about half a dozen strong were spotted hurrying away some five hundred yards from the village. They stopped in a dry river bed about one thousand yards away.

The Khattak company moved across open country under cover of mortar smoke to attack. The Japs had already got themselves out of immediate danger, and only had to continue moving east in order to escape, but they waited, hopelessly outnumbered and out classed in fire power, and took up a defensive position to engage, if necessary, the whole battalion.

At first, their efforts were treated rather lightheartedly, but when two men of D Company were wounded by unusually long range fire, the episode became deadly serious.

The Japs resisted, defying the attackers for more than an hour, and would have held out for much longer if they had not again changed their plan from defence to withdrawal. As the men of D

Company edged themselves forward to within two hundred yards, the Japanese officer decided again to run for safety. He was, it seemed to the onlookers who were watching the battle from the village, either very stupid or very brave, for he immediately exposed himself and his party to intense small arms fire at fairly short range. All were killed in a few seconds.

The battalion set about digging in for the night. Suddenly, two grenades burst almost simultaneously and a medical orderly staggered away from a house before falling mortally wounded. Mystified, the nearest soldiers moved to investigate and were met with a fusilade of bullets from the windows. In a second, there was hardly a soldier in sight. Instinctively they went to cover like rabbits and only their discarded equipment was visible to indicate their whereabouts. A few more shots rang out and the noise reverberated like claps of thunder in the narrow confines between the rows of houses.

A tricky situation had developed. The village was packed with soldiers and in their midst a number of aggressive Japs were concealed and in a murderous mood. Small arms fire would inevitably kill more friends than foes, and for a few minutes the Japs had practically a whole battalion on the defensive, but this state of affairs could not prevail for long, and presently several soldiers ventured cautiously from cover.

Vic and the C.O. edged forward to have a look; an enterprising young sepoy stood up to throw a smoke grenade at the occupied house and dived for cover as a flurry of bullets dug in the earth around him.

The little black grenade fell short, rolled a few inches and stopped, sending up a wisp of harmless smoke before it spluttered and died. There was a breathless silence, no one moved for minutes and then two more grenades thudded against the house, a small flame edged along the side, gently caressing the wooden walls, then darted away and seemed to gather more strength for the attack.

Suddenly, the flames leapt up the wall, touched the thatch in a dozen places, increased in size and shot high in the air in a crackling, roaring, hissing blaze. The roof was alight in an instant, and the troops, now on their feet, moved back against the heat, watching spellbound. The Japs sat tight within the fire that raged around them; brave, stubborn, obstinate or foolish, they did not surrender but stayed until the house was a raging roaring inferno with great sheets of flame darting high above the trees. Half the roof started to slip off. It paused with flames shooting eighty feet high into the sky and then crashed to the ground. Large burning gaps appeared in the walls, the door fell outwards and there was a crash inside the house. From out of the inferno three human figures staggered and collapsed in smouldering heaps. When the flames had died down the soldiers dispersed quietly and resumed digging.

The B eschelon transport could not get through to the battalion that night and there were only a few unappetising biscuits to eat and no whisky or rum to soothe the nerves.

It had been a worrying, irritating day, and Vic was glad to escape from it by turning in early in a bracken strewn trench dug under a house built on stilts. He had been in bed a good twenty minutes when, sensing something unusual, and hearing a queer hissing slithering noise, he felt carefully for his torch. On the earth dug from the trench, and barely a foot from his head, a thin grey snake stood on half its length, quivering in the torchlight and poised to strike. Vic felt beads of sweat on his forehead.

'Everything all right Vic?' Peter Reed's voice came from the other side. Vic couldn't reply, and felt helpless, The snake held all his attention, and he was afraid that his voice or a movement might provoke an attack. He waited, with the sweat gathering on his forehead, for what seemed an endless time but in fact was only seconds. From out of the darkness and into the light something flashed quick and bright, cutting the snake in two pieces, which wriggled convulsively until Shamroz, bayonet in hand, tossed them out into the night.

'Well done, and thanks, Shamroz,' Vic said, 'Whew! that was a near thing! I'd rather face a hundred Japs than a snake like that.'

Vic shuddered as he wondered what would have happened had he been fast asleep, and not wide awake and pondered on the discomfort of war until his eyes closed from sheer fatigue.

The advance was resumed at first light, this time at a more leisurely pace, for the going was becoming rough, and the route lay across a range of small hills. Halting just after midday, plans were at once made to attack Pyabwe, a small town twenty miles south of Meiktila, which in peacetime housed a large detachment of the Burma Military Police. It sat across the main road, possessed a main line railway station and was reported very strongly held by the enemy who, Intelligence said, included a Japanese Comfort Battalion - a female unit. Their reported presence at Pyabwe created a little more zest for the attack.

It seemed to Vic as he studied the overall plan that every soldier, gun and tank in the division was going to be involved, and that every plane in the Fourteenth Army would be in support. Two brigades were going to attack from the north, the other brigade from the south and south-west, with a squadron of Sherman tanks in hull down position on the east to stop the enemy's escape.

'This looks pretty foolproof,' Vic said to Peter Reed.

'Looks all right, but the little old Jap will probably find a way out; he usually does,' Peter replied.

'Well, if he isn't well dug in he will suffer badly from the weight of shells and bombs, but I suppose the Jap dug-outs are a mile deep as usual, damn them.'

'One thing, from our position on the ridge we will have a grandstand view,' Peter said pointing out the area on the map.

'I reckon we'll find that high ground strongly held, but when we have taken it the rest should be fairly easy.'

They had their first decent meal for a couple of days., The transport had at last come forward with food and ammunition, and the troops had already taken their evening meal and filled their water bottles.

Water was becoming a serious problem now that the battalion was moving across country, for supplies en route were unlikely, and the possibility of obtaining a sufficient quantity from the rear being brought forward by transport was remote. Thirst was enemy number two. A relatively short march in the temperature of one hundred degrees fahrenheit caused an intense craving for water. When the enemy were near and it was necessary to run and crawl, the thirst was agony. After a short time the throat became rough as sandpaper and the tongue sticky and dry.

Next morning the attack began.

Within an hour, B Company were under intense fire from Jap snipers who, dug in and well concealed on the high ground, were difficult to find, let alone dislodge. They could not be ignored, so while B Company searched and shot, A Company slipped around to the left and maintained the momentum of the advance for an hour, when they too came under heavy fire from snipers, and 75mm guns. Slowly, very slowly, and yard by yard, both companies pushed forward, finding the Japs in their deep barrel-like holes and killing them off one by one.

Gradually the high ground overlooking the main enemy position was reached and passed by the leading troops. Battalion H.Q. prepared to move up to take up a position on the reverse slope of a high ridge which at that moment was being rolled by two tanks. Along the top in a row of prickly cactus, six or seven Japs had hidden themselves, and John Smythe had asked the tanks to deal with them. Vic watched from two hundred yards, standing beside the wireless jeep, and watched the two tanks move along the skyline; he saw them stop one behind the other and rock forwards and backwards like toy rocking horses on top of the enemy foxholes.

Presently, the tanks, their job done, slithered down the slope and moved off. Vic gave the orders to the signallers and clambered in beside the driver of a jeep which stood at an alarming angle on the side of a hill.

'Keep to the side of the hill,' he said to the driver, 'and get ready to duck.'

Vic viewed the sides of the hills with some suspicion for they were covered in thick scrub and provided perfect cover for Jap snipers. The jeep dashed forward around the side of the hill at breakneck speed, with telephone spindle spinning furiously as it paid out cable and stopped between the two hills.

Battalion H.Q. started to move forward to take up position behind the ridge of high ground, and in the area where Vic stood beside the wireless jeep. Suddenly, the cactus on the top became alive. Two light machine guns chattered in long bursts toward the advancing troops at barely thirty yards range, and almost simultaneously three or four 75mm shells skidded along the ground and exploded harmlessly in the rear. Two or three Japanese riflemen joined in and while their fire was inaccurate, due perhaps to their ordeal beneath the tanks, the advance was stopped.

Vic on the right flank, and now with the signallers underneath the jeep, heard the C.O. bellow, 'Lithgow! Lithgow!' and directed his attention from the Japs to the colonel who was in a somewhat awkward predicament. His bush hat had given him away; the Japs had recognised a worthwhile target and bullets were literally peppering the ground within a few inches of his feet as he lay head down on the open ground. His body and head were in dead ground to the enemy due to the slope of the ground, but his legs and feet were exposed. The Japs had seen him go to ground. He could not move forward for grenades were bursting ahead, and he could not go back.

Vic answered his call for help. Then seeing the humour of the situation, became convulsed with laughter. At that moment the telephone which had been connected when the jeep halted rang insistently. Vic crawled around to the back and picked up the receiver.

The brigade major's voice announced, 'I've got an air strike overhead with their fuel running out. Can you give me a target quickly?'

'Can you wait for three minutes? We've just walked into some trouble with a dozen Japs thirty yards ahead, and we are pinned down for a few minutes. I'll ring you back.'

'O.K. but make it quick.' The B.M. rang off.

Vic picked up his rifle, dashed across the open ground and threw himself on the ground a dozen yards on the near and safe side of the C.O. who shouted, 'Get D Company to move those bloody Japs. Can't you see what is happening?' Vic saw all right.

The Japs were now concentrating on getting the C.O. but providing he kept still he was reasonably safe, at least for the time being. Vic, concealing his mirth dashed back to the jeep, forgetting his rifle in his hurry and immediately returned for it. Breathless he rang brigade, giving as a target for the airstrike, a group of trees about three hundred yards ahead of the leading troop. Turning back to the wireless he spoke to D Company commander.

'I'm sending in a party from H.Q. Will you move up in case we need you?'

The party, led by Shamroz, had already nipped around on the right, and as Vic left the wireless, he heard the comforting sound of tommy gun chatter and the dull explosion of grenades bursting in the deep foxholes. The handful of Japs – there were only ten - were all killed but H.Q. had sustained one killed and two wounded.

Two hundred yards ahead, the leading companies were also held up within a quarter of a mile of the enemy position by heavy and accurate fire. From overhead, the sun shone down fiercely. The sweat poured from the men. They were forced to carry their tin helmets and wore instead soft berets, which provided no protection against bullet or shell splinter but were relatively comfortable.

The metal work on the jeep and wireless sets became hot to touch, and everybody was parched with thirst. Water bottles and chagals were empty. There was no hope of supplies coming from the rear, so in desperation the reserve companies dug a well in the low ground between the two ranges of hills. A bomb had made a crater four feet deep, and a dozen men quickly dug to a depth of seven feet when a slow trickle of water oozed in from the sides. An hour later the water was a foot deep. The doctor pronounced it fit to drink, and one hundred and fifty men were able to replenish their water bottles with cool, clear water. Thus was resource rewarded.

To obviate the deadlock which threatened, an attack under an artillery barrage and with air support was laid on, but a few minutes before H hour the brigade major phoned to say that the artillery would not be available for half an hour as it was still committed on the right flank. During the waiting period, Robin London, the Battalion Second-in-Command, disappeared until he was seen sitting on the top of a mound of earth, twiddling his swagger cane about fifty yards ahead of the most forward troops. He sat quite leisurely and composed in full view of the enemy who, apparently were too surprisd to take action.

The C.O. nearly had a fit. 'Get him back before he is shot, Lithgow,' he said to Vic, adding, 'what the devil is he doing?' Vic gave a noncommittal reply and moved away quickly to busy himself with the wireless. Robin was very capable of looking after himself. He had a charmed life, and anyway, how on earth could I get him back, thought Vic.

Soon after, the artillery started, a hundred guns and mortars sent tons of high explosive into the trees which concealed the Japs. Hurricanes dive-bombed and strafed their position for thirty minutes, but when the attack started, the Japs popped up with just as much fight as ever.

Progress was slow as the Sikhs sweated their way from bush to bush, from hillock to hillock, crawling a few yards, bellies pressed flat against the warm hard earth, and then dashing recklessly across the bits of open ground. Through a thick patch of prickly scrub they moved two or three feet at a time, zigzagging between the bushes, pausing here and there to wipe the sweat from their foreheads before it rolled into their eyes.

From the darkness of the trees on the right, the Japs watched, alert, waiting with rifle and machine gun for a Sikh to expose himself, then instantly the bullets spat into the ground, and little spouts of dust shot up a few inches and then slowly drifted away. The Japs were being hit from the air by shell and mortar and from the Punjabis but they gave no sign of defeat.

Vic lay on the ground watching the whole battlefield. He saw the gun flashes and the shells bursting on the enemy, and heard the din and rumble. His rifle lay on a flat stone, and when the noise was at its highest, a lizard appeared on the same stone. It stopped, cocked its head and blinked, then, it seemed to Vic, it shrugged its little body in a gesture of resignation and ran toward the edge of the stone. It stopped suddenly, and looked back quickly and briefly, and then disappeared. Vic smiled grimly to himself.

Brigade telephoned incessantly. 'How far have you advanced?' 'Please get a move on.' 'Speed is needed, push on, seize the waterworks before darkness.' The brigade major, and the brigadier gave orders, made requests, and asked if the battalion needed more air or artillery support, and always ended the message with 'Push on! Push on!'

The Sikhs pushed on yard by yard, and eventually secured the edge of the waterworks in the rear of the enemy position. Immediately, D Company moved to a village a mile south.

Half an hour before dusk, strange orders came from brigade. The battalion were told to withdraw a thousand yards, leaving one company in position north of the waterworks, and to send patrols toward the north from D Company. Mike Boon, of the Sikhs, was furious; he had fought hard to gain his footing on the enemy position, and now the advantage was being thrown away. He protested angrily.

At the same time as this was happening, the officers and men in Battalion H.Q. had the fright of their lives. An orderly suddenly yelled 'Tanks! Tanks! Sahib,' and pointed to the east where a column of tanks were heading straight towards them. Vic watched them through his binoculars, made out eight tanks in single file, a mile away, approaching slowly. He remained, eyes glued to the glasses, saw that the leading tank had a flag flying, and then as the tanks tacked, changing course to avoid some bad ground, he recognised it as the scarlet sun of the

Japanese. Other watchers had seen it. 'They're Jap,' several muttered, and moved uneasily, but Vic wasn't sure and stood his ground.

The light was failing, the tanks were now approaching head on and recognition was impossible. He felt a spasm of acute anxiety and his heart thumped quickly. Everybody stood or lay still as the tanks drew nearer. Everyone had the jitters but kept silent, and only the rumble of the approaching tanks churning their way nearer and nearer could be heard.

If they are Japs we must move quickly, thought Vic, but they haven't got any tanks in the area. Or have they? We don't really know. We can move quickly for cover, but where? If we run and they are our own tanks, we shall look bloody silly. The thoughts flashed one after the other through his mind. He opened his mouth to give an order. He stood with it open as the nearest tank slewed around and stopped broadside on fifty yards away. It was a Sherman.

A head appeared from a hole on the top and a voice shouted, 'We thought you were Japs! Cheerio.' A hand waved, and the tank lumbered on, followed by seven more, one behind the other like huge ducks waddling to water, their outline shadowy in the twilight.

'There should be a law against this sort of thing, Vic,' said Peter Reed weakly, 'I've never been so scared in my life.'

Vic received details of the fighting by other units in the division. Good progress had been made, a lot of Japs had been killed by the same tanks which had caused the scare. Having taken up hull down positions at dawn behind the railway embankment, they had waited patiently all day, until just after 1600 hours when a party of Japs over two hundred strong had approached, moving in close formation. The enemy had marched straight towards the tanks and all had been killed within a few minutes.

Shamroz appeared with the enamel mug. Vic drank and felt better as the neat Scotch whisky revived him, casting out the tiredness which had crept through his mind and body. Refreshed, he turned to the signallers and asked them to get the news on the wireless.

In a few moments a voice, calm and unemotional, announced the details of the fighting at Pyawbwe. Vic and Peter listened intently as the voice went on, 'the thirst was so great that our men in close contact drank water from a hole in the ground, water which seeped through the mud as the men waited. One well was actually dug during battle.' Vic could hardly believe his ears. 'Did you hear that, Peter?' he asked.

'Yes, but it can't be us, but. . . ' he left the sentence unfinished his face incredulous.

'Two battalions must have dug for water today, I wonder who the other one was?' Vic said.

In almost total darkness, the officers ate the tinned stew and when the meal was over, a deep silence crept over the acre of ground between the two sharp hills which sheltered the five hundred men. It was a still night and the air was soft and čol. The moon had not as yet climbed over the hills.

It was a comforting darkness to Vic, lying between two blocks of stone, his hands behind his head and puffing gently on his pipe. He was exhausted and in a minute or so he carefully tapped the ashes out on the stone, blew through the pipe, put it in his haversack and turned over to sleep.

A few hours later, in the half light of the dawn, the Pathans of D Company crept cautiously up the slope from the south, halted when they reached the top, and then moved forward again down the hill and through the waterworks.

There were two or three sharp outbursts of noise and subdued chatter as here and there a few men stopped to look quickly at the groups of dead Japanese. It had already been obvious to the company commander that the waterworks were undefended; the enemy who had escaped the fury of the previous day's fighting had moved out under the cover of darkness, but they left behind adequate evidence of their defeat. Alas, the comfort battalion was not seen.

When the rest of the battalion moved down to link up with D Company, the Sikhs found a prisoner of war. He was a miserable little man with a wisp of goatee beard and a badly shattered leg which had prevented him from escaping with his few comrades. Menaced by half a dozen Sikhs whom Mike Boon had some difficulty in restraining, for they appeared anxious to kill him, he protested volubly, chattering ninety to the dozen.

The event was significant. He was a prisoner of war, and although his wounds may have prevented his movement, they did not form a sufficient reason for not committing hari kiri. The total of two hundred and two Jap bodies found in the area included many whose death was self-inflicted, and like many seen before, had ugly holes in their stomachs.

There were few individual foxholes except on the outskirts of the position, but on the fringe of the trees there were many large bunkers and dug outs linked by deep underground tunnels. Some of the earthworks were large enough to hold a truck and were covered with six feet of earth, which in several cases was supported on logs of timber a foot thick. The tunnels were wide enough for two men to walk abreast and there was no indication that our artillery or bombing had penetrated the shelters, but the trees were badly scarred and branches hung loosely and swung gently in the breeze. The air was thick with decay; a nauseating smell of staleness, of rotting bodies and unclean habitations.

Orders came to stand fast for twenty four hours and the cleaning of the area, weapons, men and clothes commenced with vigour. Soon the unholy stench disappeared. The area became a more pleasant spot and the men, stripped to the waist, worked with a will. The trees and bushes were soon festooned with clothes hanging out to dry. There was plenty of water; hopeful eyes were cast at the swimming pool which, because it contained Japanese corpses, was placed out of bounds.

Typewriters worked overtime in Battalion Headquarters, and Vic got down to the task of typing the numerous citations for immediate decorations. Company commanders had been asked for their recommendations as soon as the halt was called. About thirty men had distinguished themselves and since only two, or three at the most, would receive awards, it was necessary to preserve absolute secrecy. Vic worked alone late into the night, laboriously, with two fingers, in one of the timbered bunkers which had been cleaned out and illuminated by a small bulb wired to a tank battery.

Next morning, all ranks were awake and dressed at dawn, and the officers assembled on the grassy high ground for breakfast. From where they sat, the road to Rangoon could be seen running straight, like a thin long pencil, for four or five miles. Parked on either side were hundreds of vehicles, tiny in the distance like matchboxes, and packed tight together in rows for as far as the eye could see. The vehicles belonged, at least for the time being, to the 5th Indian Division which had passed through 17th Division. The rival division were now in the lead. Their 'tail' only just cleared Pyawbwe, but they were undoubtedly ahead.

'Five Division are slow getting off the mark this morning,' Vic said.

'They don't seem to be awake yet, there is no movement around the trucks,' Peter joined in. 'They will never get to Rangoon at this rate, not before the monsoon, anyway,' he added.

'They seem to have some air support, can you see those planes, over there, look!' Vic replied, pointing to the south.

About a dozen fighters were approaching in tight formation at ten thousand feet or thereabouts. They wheeled suddenly, changed formation and dived, bombing the vehicles.

'Hells bells!' shouted Vic suddenly, 'they're Jap Zeros, and boy oh boy, what a time they are going to have. There isn't an ack-ack gun within miles.'

From their vantage point, the group of officers watched the Zeros bomb and machine gun the halted column in what seemed to them a leisurely manner. In a few moments several trucks were on fire and the Japs moved their attack to a point further along the road, and then having apparently expended their bombs and ammunition, reformed in mid-air and flew off to the south.

'There will be an even greater shortage of transport now,' Peter said.

Vic walked over to the command post where a despatch rider was turning out a fair sized mail bag. Vic suddenly exclaimed, 'Heavens! The General is coming at 1030, I had better tell the C.O. and warn the companies.' And Vic moved over to where the colonel was talking to the subadar major.

Vic passed the message and paused to chat with Firoz Khan, the battalion subadar major, who was in a very benign mood. Rotund, always cheerful, a fund of information, quite ageless, for this was his second world war, Firoz was the senior Viceroy's Commissioned Officer, and the battalion's greatest asset. He was the C.O.'s adviser on religion, which in a unit made up of Sikhs, Pathans, Punjabis, Jats, and Madrasis, was of vital importance, but he held the reins gently in firm hands, and squabbles between Hindu and Muslim or other religions were unknown. All classes worked and fought together as a team, all pulling together. A Khattak (Muslim) himself, he possessed an uncanny flair for impartiality, and was a true friend of every officer and man.

The general brought good news and bad. His obviously very sincere thanks to all ranks for their efforts during the past weeks were good to hear, and hearts warmed to him. But then he disclosed that the battalion would become the divisional defence battalion, with effect, from the following day.

Bad news indeed! For the role of the new job was merely the defence of division and brigade headquartrs, involving a breaking up of the unit into companies and sub-units, and, it appeared, a loss in prestige.

The 6th Punjabis had suffered very heavy losses, their strength was below half their original number, reinforcements in the quantity required were not expected and so, the general explained, he had decided that for the time being, the battalion would undertake a less arduous task. The depressing news cast a shadow of gloom over all ranks and none felt it more keenly than Vic and Robin, who were to assume the appointments of staff captain and officer commanding, respectively, of the divisional administration base, which was to remain for a while at Pyawbwe.

Later that afternoon, the gloom lifted when Ian Stewart, the brigade major, telephoned with the glad tidings that the battalion had been awarded two Military Crosses, and two Military Medals. Both the M.C.s were for B Company, to John Smythe and Jemadar Lal Khan, for their valour at Meiktila. Both were so richly deserved, and were celebrated during the evening in customary manner. Vic wondered at the fate of the dozen more citations that had been submitted.

The next day Vic, with the other members of the headquarters, stood with sad heart watching the rifle companies embus in borrowed trucks and depart one after the other to their new jobs. When they had all gone, the place was empty. The remnants of the battalion made their way over the hill on foot to the south, and occupied some very battered and bombed but, notwithstanding, relatively comfortable wooden barracks.

The race for Rangoon had not stopped, nor had the momentum slackened, for barely three weeks of dry weather remained and time was now short.

Colonel Smedley was suddenly promoted to a staff appointment at Div. H.Q. and Robin London was promoted to colonel and commanding officer.

10

TO RANGOON

When the 5th Division took over the lead in the race to Rangoon, there was little reason for the optimistic spirit which infected the men of both Divisions. There was over three hundred miles between the advance troops and Rangoon; the weather would break for certainty in three weeks, and possibly in only two if the fates were unkind and the monsoon came early. The road itself was metalled and quite good by Burmese standards, but it had been neglected and was full of potholes. It was narrow and two vehicles could pass only with difficulty. But it was good enough.

Desperate as well as fanatical, the Japanese were determined to hang on to their Burmese possessions and prepared to fight to the last. It was doubtful if they were aware of their true position for, even in Burma, three hundred miles is a long way.

The capture of Rangoon was vital to the Allies; the very existence of the 14th Army depended on the opening of Burma's main port, and the consequences of failure were unthinkable. If Rangoon was not captured, then the Army would become bogged down in the mud, very vulnerable to enemy attack, and unless a miracle happened, would be without supplies. Some food and stores were coming in by road and river but these were negligible. The bulk had been flown in from Imphal, which became further out of range as the advance continued south. The potential base of Ramree had been captured in January and there were others, but while these were suitable in the dry season, most of the air bases would be quite useless during the monsoon. Unless Rangoon was captured before the rain started, disaster on the largest scale seemed inevitable.

The words 'On to Rangoon!' were on everybody's lips day in and day out, not as a slogan, nor as an order, but as something much more profound, signifying the single-minded purpose of every man. It was do or die, Rangoon or bust. This spirit tore through the entire force like a fever, sweeping aside personal thoughts and discomforts and holding the imagination in a vice-like grip. Every thought and action of every man was provoked and designed to speed the race and beat the rains. Nothing else mattered, other things were irrevelant. The shortage of water, of rations, and the fierce Burma sun became of no account. It was a race for survival, against defeat, against starvation.

In this, their finest hour, the men of the 14th Army neither scowled nor even frowned. Their unquenchable spirit brought forth their best. They smiled and grinned, and whilst the world at large looked askance at the Eastern Front, they argued one with another not if when, but When? The General had said 'We'll be in Rangoon by May '45,' way back in November '44, and now with two-thirds of the journey over and many battles won, the 14th Army was on the last lap.

Ahead lay a long road, no jungle to speak of and the weather was fine and dry, but the Japs were not done and at Yamethin, Pyinmana and at Toungoo, there was a series of sharp actions which delayed the advance. At several places enemy snipers resisted until their last round was spent. On the flanks and off the road, Japanese columns and patrols moved to the south and east. On one occasion, friend and foe advanced within sight of each other on parallel lines, the Allies with armoured and motorised columns on the road, and the enemy trudging on foot along the lower slopes of the foothills.

Only those Japs who impeded the advance justified attention. There was no time for the rest. On one occasion John Smythe of the 6th Punjabis found himself and his company escorting a forward troop of armoured cars when an enemy force four hundred odd strong was seen on the flank. John reported to Brigade H.Q. and asked what he should do.

'Do! Do! John? If they are not on the road, for heaven's sake leave 'em alone and get on to Rangoon!' The Brigadier had exploded.

The audacious, perilous advance raced on. Meanwhile, the 6th Punjabis H.Q. languished at Pyawbwe.

Vic was ordered to send vital supplies forward to 17th

Division but he had no motor transport. Fortunately, the main railway line ran alongside almost the whole road to Rangoon and someone, with great ingenuity, had arranged to use the railway for the purpose of transporting supplies from the base at Meiktila to the advancing troops. The railway lines, which had been bombed in a score of places suddenly became fit for traffic. Sufficient wagons were found and rapidly made serviceable but there were no engines, a fact which might have been serious but it neither delayed nor hindered the operation. The wheelbase of the standard jeep was found to be exactly the same gauge as the track and, without tyres, fitted the lines perfectly.

On day one, Vic and Peter supervised the loading of three railway wagons at Meiktila with about one hundred tons of supplies. Three jeeps in tandem were linked to pull the load which they could do very effectively. But there was one problem – when travelling downhill, the train was difficult to stop as the momentum of the load tended to over-run the jeeps!

As the first train pulled away, Vic suddenly remembered that there was an unmanned crossing at Pyawbwe and that the road was heavily congested with military traffic. 'My God,' he exclaimed, 'we must get to Pyawbwe and stop the traffic before the train arrives.' His vision of the train ploughing through army trucks was frightening.

He and Peter set off in the jeep at breakneck speed, mostly on the road but frequently on the verges, over ditches and paddy fields. They cut off corners, passed trucks on the right side and often on the wrong side. Other drivers cursed and shook their fists but Vic raced on with horn blaring continuously. The jeep bucked and skidded alarmingly but the engine did not stall, and they arrived just in time to put the jeep broadside across the road. The traffic had to stop and there were strong protests; but not for long, for within a minute or so the train moved sedately across the road and disappeared carrying its load of precious supplies. A major of the Indian Engineers who was in the leading truck passed his hand over his eyes in disbelief, 'I have seen everything now,' he muttered as he walked away.

Thereafter, the 'train' was organised, and Pyawbwe became a second Kings Cross and for several weeks supplies were sent forward on a most satisfactory basis.

Down the Rangoon road the advance, after a hesitant start from Pyawbwe, was gaining momentum and on 22 April,

Toungoo was captured much to the surprise of the Japanese Kempai Tai Unit (Military Police) who guarded an internment camp.

The story went the rounds of how a member of the Kempai Tai, on traffic duty, stood in the middle of the road and raised his hand to halt the leading car. His assumption that the car was Japanese was fatal. Conjecture on what the policeman would have done had the car driver merely halted and shown his identification as a British driver, caused quite a few cynical grins. His surprise was not unexpected, however, for the swiftness of the dash south had completely disrupted the enemy communications.

Time was running short, the rains could be expected within ten days and the objective was still one hundred and forty miles away. The 'Black Cats' (17th Division) were impatient and apprehensive, for their rivals of the 5th Indian Division were still firmly in the lead. Three questions loomed very large. Would the race be won? Would 17th Division win the race? Or would another formation be first into Rangoon? Nothing else mattered.

There was no need for the men of 17th Division to be anxious. The leading armoured cars of 5th Division probed south to Pyu at milestone 134 on 24 April. On the next day, 17th Division swept through their lines and into the lead. Two brigades were fully mobile but 99 brigade, who had flown into battle, had barely enough vehicles for their essential supplies and stores, but they could not be left behind and improvisation became the order of the day. Tank transporters dumped their tanks and started a ferry service, bringing 99 brigade forward. While the other two brigades, and 63rd Indian, forged ahead, the tank carriers rumbled up and down the road in the sweltering heat long into the night, their broad and long platforms packed tight with troops. It was dangerous but quick.

On 28 April, the leading troops met stiff enemy opposition, but the enemy were swept aside, and the advance drove on. By the evening of the next day, 63 brigade were ready to attack Pegu. The day had been memorable for, during the advance, four hundred and twenty Allied P.O.Ws were met at Haung Pattaya. Among them was a senior medical officer who, in 1942, had served in the 17th Indian Division. The prisoners had moved out of Rangoon gaol under escort, but their Japanese guards on hearing the news of the Allied advance, had fled.

It seemed then that the race was over for the prize was barely ninety minutes motoring time away and undefended, but Pegu, which guarded the enemy escape route to the east, bristled with Japs; every available soldier had been mustered to hold the town and every bridge had been prepared for demolition. It was here, fifty one miles from Rangoon, that the enemy made his last stand. Early on May Day, the 'Black Cats' attacked.

They had travelled a long way from the heights of Imphal and Palel, through the Kabaw Valley and on to the Central Plains and Meiktila, down the road to Rangoon, smashing the enemy at Pyawbwe and a dozen other places. Now within sight of complete victory, they threw everything into the attack and fought like men possessed, but their courage and skill were not enough. The Japs blew up the bridge across the Pegu river and the advance was halted.

While the battle continued unabated on the flanks, and sometimes close at hand, the engineers worked like demons to fling a pontoon bridge across the broad expanse of water, but a day had been lost, and then; the rains came. Within an hour the river became a deep raging torrent and the new bridge was swept down river. About half the division had crossed before the bridge was lost, so the other half were marooned on the north side. The river overflowed its banks, making the approaches almost impassable. While the engineers toiled and fought against mud and water, the leading elements of the division pressed on towards its goal, but, the race was lost. The halt for a day had cost the division an advance of fifty miles. Rangoon was fifty one miles away.

On 5 May, when the enemy had ceased to count and when only thirty miles of clear unmined road lay ahead, and when Rangoon, quite undefended, was so near, new orders were received. The 14th Army would not go to Rangoon! It was a bitter blow which shattered morale and bruised the spirit. Denied their lawful prize at the eleventh hour, and after so many difficulties had been overcome, the men of the 17th Division, in particular, and of 4 Corps in general, felt cheated and bitter.

Whilst they cursed the occupation of Rangoon was being completed. It had been occupied by other Allied troops.

Sea-borne landings had taken place on 2 May, the day after

the attack on Pegu. The Japanese evacuation had taken place several days previously. An R.A.F. Wing Commander had made a forced landing on a Rangoon airfield and was there to greet the 'invasion' force. He had already been to visit the remaining Allied prisoners of war in the jail and learned from them that they had painted the message 'Japs Gone' on their prison roof, and later, when this had apparently been ignored by the R.A.F. had changed the words to 'Extract Digit', thinking that the prisoners' first message had been taken for a Japanese trick. The second message left no room for doubt.

To the ordinary soldier and indeed to many officers, the assault on the undefended capital seemed to be unnecessary and a gross waste of war power. It would have been much more profitable, they argued, if the assault had been against Moulmein, the only port now in enemy hands, and to where the escaping Japanese were now heading. With Moulmein in Allied hands, the fate of thousands more Japs would have been sealed. The enemy still retained a bridgehead in Burma.

The morale of the 14th Army sagged for a day or so, and then returned to normal as operations were resumed against the Japanese 15th and 28th Armies who were trapped north of the capital and who were now preparing to cross the Sittang river and escape to Moulmein.

The rivalry between 17th and 5th Indian Division was friendly, but the feeling expressed by these two divisions against the 'usurpers' at Rangoon was strong. It was best summed up by the story which spread rapidly from unit to unit during the middle of May, which was probably quite unrelated to the truth but indicated the attitude of the men of 4 Corps to those of 15 Corps. The commander of the latter, so the tale went, living in the height of luxury in Government House, Rangoon, invited the commander of 4 Corps, who was living in discomfort and fighting in the monsoon, to dinner. The reply was brief. 'Thanks for your kind invitation stop regret unable to accept stop am dealing with 30,000 Japs who left Rangoon on the day you left India.'

11

THE START OF THE BREAKOUT

At the time, the capture of Rangoon was vital and perhaps the seaborne invasion was justified on the grounds of ensuring its capture before the monsoon broke, but the facts show that the Japs had fled a few days previously and, therefore, the achievement of the seaborne landing was limited.

North of Rangoon, between thirty thousand and forty thousand Japanese are cut off and the 14th Army now turn about and advance north up the road away from Rangoon to smash the enemy's attempt to move east and escape across the Sittang River. Fighting in many widely scattered places continues for three weeks as the Japanese try to fight their way out of the traps. But a large force, the enemy's 28th Army from the Arakan, concentrate in the depths of the Pegu Yomas hills, which are thickly wooded and provide perfect cover. Without stores and supplies, and existing on their limited reserve food, and on whatever they could gain from the land, the Japanese army remain in their wooded retreat day after day, week after week. It was not until the end of June, eight weeks after the fall of Rangoon that they ventured forth.

On 1 June, the battalion concentrated at Nyaungbintha, at milestone 128 on the Rangoon-Meiktila road, to prepare for the approaching escape bid by the Japanese. They were preparing to escape by crossing the main road and the Sittang river into Thailand.

The battalion was given a stretch of road about ten miles long, with orders to kill all Japs who attempted to cross it. A few parties of Japs had already crossed the road prior to the battalion's arrival, and on all these occasions they had hidden in the foothills in the west by day and then moved by night under the guidance of locals past the British positions. Then they had hidden in the villages between the main road and the Sittang river on the following day and moved east again after darkness.

The C.O. planned to carry out what seemed at first an impossible task. The battalion was about half its normal strength, and only had about five hundred men to cover the ten miles. In addition, the C.O. had, in support, the 493 Field Battery from Liverpool, one platoon of the Frontier Force Machine Gun Regiment, and one company from the 6th Rajput Anti Tank Regiment.

Opposite Nyaungbintha, on the west of the road, there was an area of low but dense jungle. North and south of the jungle there was fairly open country and it seemed obvious that if the Japs intended to cross the road through the battalion sector they would approach along the track which ran through the ford and jungle and on to the road. The country on the east of the road was flat and open; it was covered to a large extent with water varying in depth from a few inches near the road to several feet near the Sittang.

It was estimated that the total strength of the enemy was in the region of thirty thousand of whom it was assumed that a fair number would die from hunger and exhaustion. The task of watching such a colossal area and dealing with the Japs who attempted to escape presented some problems. It was safe to assume that the enemy would move in fairly large parties and, therefore, a wide dispersal of the battalion could not be considered. Movement on foot through the flooded countryside was slow, extremely tiring, and likely to cause foot-rot, which might easily put the whole battalion out of action in a short time.

It was inevitable that many men would suffer from this painful complaint. Feet would become wet and stay wet for periods of up to twenty four hours, and sometimes longer. In addition the area was highly malarious. Rigid precautions were enforced immediately, including the frequent spraying of bivouacs, and the wearing of headnets on night operations. All ranks were innoculated against cholera, which had claimed a few local Burmese.

Within two days the part of Nyaungbintha which was occupied began to look like a strong defensive position. The men seemed inspired and worked hard and continuously from dawn to dusk for most of the time in heavy rain. Nyaungbintha

'Box' was in two parts, being divided by a swamp of black mud seventy yards wide, which ran from north to south. To the east lay the village of Nyaungbintha which was partially occupied by Burmese, who at once became good friends of all ranks, and started a mutually profitable business in cheroots, eggs, poultry and rice.

A patrol from another battalion killed a small Jap patrol and captured the enemy operation order for the breakout, which indicated that the main movement of the Jap 28th Army across the main road would start at the end of June, and that a substantial number intended to pass through the sector held by the 6th Punjabis. The enemy movements seemed to confirm the approximate date, so it was assumed that there were less than ten days to go before the outbreak of an intensive battle. Many officers within the division who voiced their scepticism, describing the captured operation order as a ruse to deceive, and one senior commanding officer, in particular, voiced his conviction in no uncertain manner at a C.O.'s conference. He felt that the time was about right, for the moon would be full and conditions suitable for mass movement, but was sure that the main crossing would take place in an area sixteen miles further south. He should have known better.

Later, when Robin London gave this vital information to his assembled officers, he expressed his own strong disagreement. His officers felt likewise.

'There is every indication that large parties of Japs will pass through our area,' he said. 'We must all be on the alert at all times. There is a strong possibility that the Jap will attack our position and thus clear the way for a mass escape through this area. The enemy outnumber us by perhaps forty or fifty to one.'

'Patrols will be increased immediately, and more attention paid to hygiene, in particular, to foot-rot. How many sick have we got now, Doctor?'

'There were twenty this morning with bad foot-rot.'

'You must get them better quickly. We can't afford to have nearly a platoon off duty at the present time.'

The doctor, who was very popular and well thought of by all, was a little embarrassed.

'It's all very well sir,' he protested gently, 'but the only cure or, for that matter, a preventative for foot-rot, is dry feet and the men just cannot keep dry unless they are excused duty. The issued foot powder helps a lot but we don't get sufficient, and I cannot get any more.'

'All right, Doc. After lunch, borrow my jeep, go down to Divisional H.Q., see the most senior medical officer and give him the facts. If you cannot get any more foot powder, get permission to buy talcum from the canteen. I take it that talcum powder will do the trick?'

The Doc smiled gratefully.

Vic stayed behind with the C.O. who said to him, 'I must say everybody is keen and enthusiastic.'

'Yes, sir. We all think a lot of Japs will come our way. Apparently, the official appreciation is different. It's going to be very pleasant proving the brains utterly wrong.'

Vic spoke confidently.

'You sound very sure,' Robin said.

'Well, everything points to a big break out right through the middle of our sector. There's the ford in the river, and the jungle, just across the road, all our patrol reports, and the captured operation order which I believe is genuine. It all adds up.'

For the next few days parties of Japs were seen frequently in the foothills west of the Kun Chaung but there was no movement across the river.

Towards the end of the month, the battalion received some help, at least in number, when a whole battalion of the Burmese Peoples Independence Army was placed at the C.O.'s disposal. A fresh-faced well-built major of Force 136* drove his jeep into the position one afternoon, asked to see the commanding officer and replied to Vic's question on the nature of his business that he had a battalion of good soldiers to spare. Vic, who was sitting in the tiny command post, stubbed out his cheroot, put on his tunic, and invited the major to tea.

The idea of assistance appealed to him but he felt suspicious. 'Who are these soldiers?' he asked.

'They are a battalion of General Aung San's Army. You know, of course, that he is now fighting for us instead of against us!'

Vic gave a derisive laugh, 'Come off it, old man, you are not

*The title given to SOE (Special Operations Executive in S.E. Asia.)

being serious! Why only recently they were fighting our troops, not very effectively I know, but surely you don't expect us to have anything to do with that crowd? Why the dickens S.E.A.C. accepted a turncoat like Aung San, I just can't imagine. The place for him and his army is behind bars. They fought against us for years while we were being driven back, then, when we start to win, Mr. Aung San and his People's Army say to the Allies, 'We are sorry we fought against you, please accept our apologies and treat us as friends and we will help you to drive the accursed Jap out of our country.' Vic acted as he spoke, portraying oriental gesturs. The major grinned.

'Oh, it's not as bad as that! I have been here during most of the Jap occupation and the battalion I am offering you has only just been formed. True, they belong to the People's Army but they are all locals and have not fought before as a unit. They could at least do some patrols for you.'

The major was a very decent type and Vic warmed to him as he made his case. He was, after all, a member of Force 136, his face was sincere and he was earnest. As the discussion continued, Vic changed his mind.

'All right,' he said, 'you have convinced me, and I think the C.O. will agree too but only on the understanding that the unit remains at Pyu and is completely under our command for operations. We will supply ammunition and medical supplies, both of which will be strictly rationed. O.K.?'

'O.K.' grinned the major.

Robin London agreed, suggesting that the People's Army would be useful for long range patrols, particularly on the northern boundary.

Next morning, the Burmese C.O. reported. He was young, not much more than twenty, was pleasant and seemed efficient, with a very engaging manner.

'Will you come and have a meal with me soon?' he asked Vic after their discussion.

'We are very busy at the moment, but many thanks,' Vic had tried to be pleasant.

They parted company, the Burmese C.O. by jeep back to his H.Q. at Pyu, with a thousand rounds of .303 which he had been told must last a month, and Vic to the R.A.P. where he found the doctor dealing with local men, women and children, who stood in a queue twenty yards long.

'Good heavens, Doc, what goes on? Plague?'

'No, just a few patients. You know its official policy now to help these people. I spoke to the headman a day or so ago and news travels fast. I've got several patients here from Pyu. One is my interpreter,' he said with a sly grin.

'She is not Burmese. Why, she is quite white!' exclaimed Vic.

'American father, Burmese mother. She is very well educated. She had a bad time in Taungoo internment camp and has been coming for treatment for several days.'

The doctor spoke almost offhandedly and resumed examining a patient.

'Doc,' Vic declared, 'you are a dark horse. She is young and damned attractive. I suppose you are keeping her to yourself!'

'No, no, Vic, you know me.'

'I'll introduce you and then you can ask her to lunch or something,' the Doc said hastily.

'No Doc, I'll leave her in your good hands. How many of our men reported sick this morning?'

'Seventeen, all with foot-rot, but I reckon that six will be back on duty within a week. I think the talcum powder is showing results.'

'Let me see, you got two hundred tins, enough for one tin between two men. You had better order some more, make it four hundred tins this time,' Vic said.

'But Vic, we are going to get into trouble. Div. H.Q. said we could purchase only in emergency but they didn't give any written authority. The canteen manager is not very keen to accept another chit in payment, and you know I have had a lot of complaints from other units because we took the entire stock. No one else can get any for a week.'

'Don't worry Doc, we signed for it, and I'll give you a chit next time, and come with you if you want some help. And for heaven's sake forget the other units! They aren't doing patrolling on anything like the same scale.'

'Well, if you say so, but there will be trouble, you mark my words,' Doc replied in a gloomy voice.

'I must go and see what is happening in the command post. Look after your glamour girl. Cheerio.'

On 28 June, the Jap made his first real attempt to cross the Kun Chaung, and contrary to expectation, it was during the afternoon. A patrol of Sikhs moving along the Pegu Yomas foothills, some two hundred yards from the Chaung spotted a party of about sixty who were marching west carrying bamboos, which indicated that they intended to cross the river on rafts.

D Company hurried to the spot through torrential rain. Approaching cautiously, they saw the Japs on the far bank making rafts. Keeping his own troops concealed in positions from where they could cover the Japs, the company commander wirelessed for artillery. In a few minutes, some forty 25lb shells exploded on the raft makers, who, surprised and shaken by the sudden attack, dashed in panic back towards the trees. The Khattaks of D Company hastened them on their way with a hail of small arms fire, and when the Japs had run about two hundred yards and felt perhaps out of immediate danger, they stopped. Another salvo fell among them and soon the survivors disappeared into the darkness of the forest. A score of bodies remained.

That evening when the officers were playing poker, the sound of small arms firing was heard, mostly from the direction of the Burmese battalion.

'Bang goes our thousand rounds,' Robin London said feelingly.

'Let's hope they get a few Japs,' Vic replied.

Three shots went off very loudly, and very near. The light flickered and the door of the hut rattled. There was a pause in playing, barely perceptible, and the game continued very quietly as if everyone was listening. Bids were made in voices barely above a whisper for a few minutes. Then the C.O. broke the tension and in a loud sharp voice demanded, 'What the Devil's the matter with us. It's only an odd Jap or two on patrol trying to find the size and strength of our position.'

There was another loud shot and its noise and echo reverberated around the small wooden hut, and the door and shutters rattled again alarmingly. The light flickered violently but survived and became still. Vic hoped the others could not hear his heart thumping. The backs of his hands tingled. Someone went to investigate, and quickly returned to confirm the C.O.'s opinion that a Jap patrol had been on the perimeter. Having failed to provoke return fire, it had departed into the darkness.

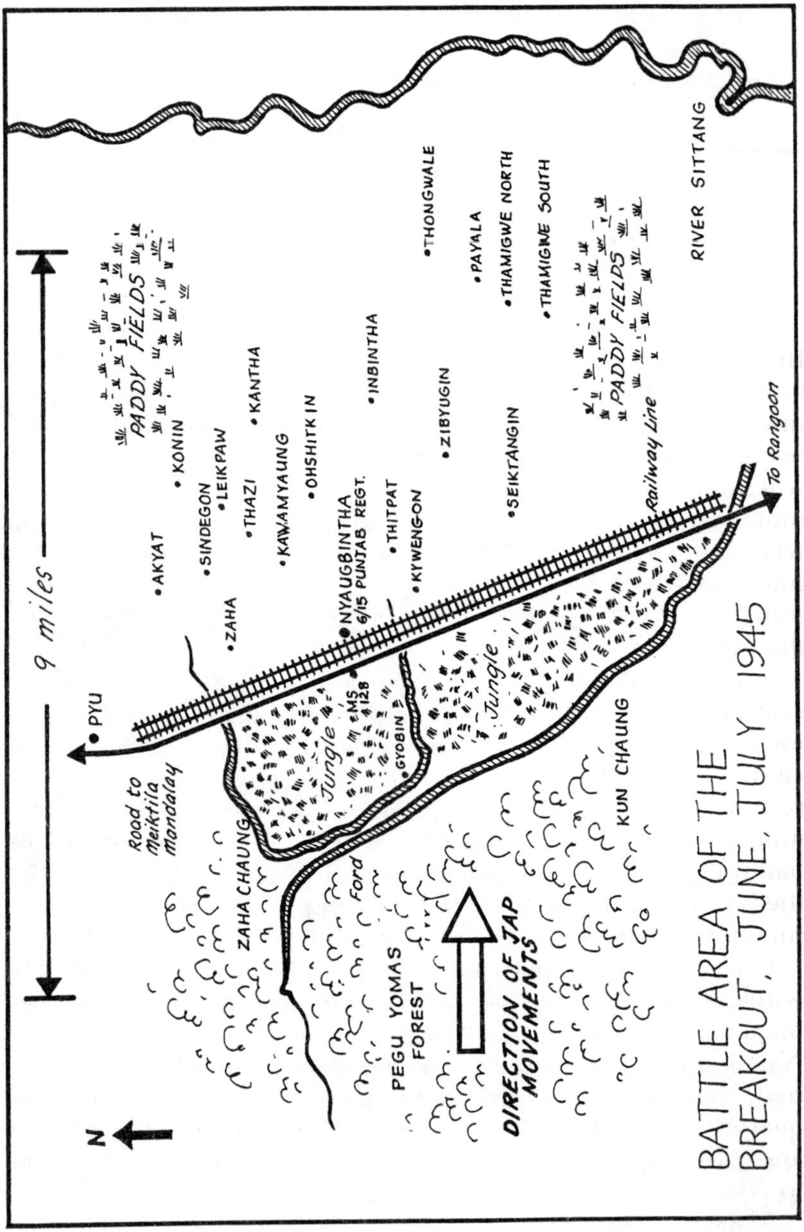

BATTLE AREA OF THE BREAKOUT, JUNE, JULY 1945

12

THE 'BREAKOUT'

In pelting rain, patrolling Sikhs searched the Pegu Yomas foothills. They met a local man who, with the help of an interpreter, informed Mike Boon that about forty Japanese had been killed by the shelling on 28 June. Late the following night when the Sikh patrol, battering its way through a slashing monsoon storm, almost walked into a large enemy force who were hurrying along a track which ran diagonally across the track on which the Sikhs were moving. The rain hissed and stung as the men, their bodies bent almost double, forced themselves along.

Suddenly, there was a new sound, alien to the hissing of the rain and the murmurs of the jungle. The patrol froze in their footsteps and listened. Away ahead and slightly to the right, came the low grumble of many tramping men. The noise receded and the Sikhs moved on to investigate. At the track junction there was a mass of footmarks. Mike's leading section had missed the tail end of the Jap column by a few yards, and if the Japs had been two or three minutes later, or the patrol a few minutes earlier, friend and foe would have met face to face.

It was too late to shoot, so Mike tried to warn his H.Q. by wireless. The enemy were making for the road. It was the first major escape bid or an attacking force on the way to Nyaungbintha. The warning must be sent quickly. Cursing his bad luck, Mike made frantic attempts to contact his headquarters, but the obstinate '68' set only crackled, whistled and spluttered, and reluctantly he gave the order to return to Nyaungbintha.

Mike realised that he could still arrange an ambush from headquarters providing that he could get a message through in time. His signallers kept calling as they marched and, at last, to Mike's relief, an answering call came when they were just over half a mile from base.

There was a poker game in progress in the Mess,and a gust of laughter went up as Doc, with a pair of nines finally outbluffed Vic, who had held a pair of aces, when the duty officer burst in.

'Mike is on the blower, it's urgent,' he exclaimed breathlessly. Vic was beside the wireless in a flash.

'Am about one thousand yards away due east. A party of Japs about six hundred strong is heading for the culvert. Can you cut them off?' asked Mike.

Vic felt his blood tingle.

Vic dashed off to the mess. With the aid of the map from the command post table, he passed the message to the C.O.

'I need a well-armed officer patrol to ambush the Jap at the culvert,' the C.O. said quickly.

There was a silence for perhaps a second and then Vic, unable to restrain himself said, 'I'll go sir,' and immediately regretted it.

'Well done,' replied the C.O. quietly.

Vic called an orderly. 'My salaams to Jemadar sahib. I need a V.C.O. and ten men from D Company with two L.M.G.s., two riflemen and the rest, tommygunners.'

Then to the signals officer, 'Will you lay on a wireless set? We may be able to call for guns or mortars.'

Vic dashed to his bivouac. 'Shamroz,' he called, 'We are going out, hurry!'

Within a few minutes, Shamroz appeared fully dressed, and helped Vic on with his equipment. 'Boots, Sahib?' he asked.

'No time,' Vic said. Shamroz grunted disapproval.

A voice outside called, 'Ready, Sahib?'

The patrol set off at a quick pace. In single file they moved along behind the cover of the railway embankment, making as little noise as possible as they trudged over the muddy ground.

A five minute monsoon storm drenched them to the skin. He calculated that the Jap would cross the road at the culvert a mile and a half ahead, and therefore he could take chances for a good mile. They hurried on, squelching and splashing for fifteen minutes; then he called a halt and gave the order to go carefully, in bounds, and to stop four hundred yards ahead. The patrol moved on quietly and slowly, their bodies merged in the shadow of the embankment. They halted. Vic and Shamroz moved forward, stopped and listened.

For a few seconds there was absolute quiet and then a bird squawked, penetratingly, startling them momentarily. 'Phew,' Vic breathed his relief. 'Stay here,' he said to the man behind, 'We're going on.'

He and Shamroz moved forward fifty yards in leap-frog fashion, and stopped and listened again. Vic thought they must be within a hundred yards of the culvert, and carefully on all fours, climbed up through the tall wet grass, on the embankment. On the top there was a narrow path, and along this Shamroz and Vic crept stealthily, keeping well down below the tops of the grass, which grew three feet high on either side.

Suddenly, they stopped and sniffed. A strong odour fouled the fresh evening air. Their hearts beat violently. It was the smell of sweaty bodies and dirty clothing. Like two pointers, Vic and Shamroz crouched, listening intently, their eyes searching the pathway ahead for a sign of movement. In the pale moonlight, Vic saw that the line of the tall grass was broken about ten yards ahead. There was a gap a yard wide where the grass had been flattened. Someone had sat there recently; someone might still be sitting there. It was the obvious place for an enemy sentry guarding a party of his own soldiers crossing the road further down.

Vic and Shamroz thought alike, and without a word or gesture, they eased themselves down the embankment to the lower ground and crept along in complete silence towards the gap. As they reached the spot, Vic motioned Shamroz to stop. Quite cool now, he fixed his bayonet, slowly parted the dripping grass and, taking the weight of his body on one hand, carefully and very slowly lay down on the wet earth. Without noise or movement of the grass, he started to move upwards toward his objective, flat on his stomach. The ten or twelve feet took him about five minutes. On reaching the flat top he paused, and slowly pushed his rifle forward to part the grass. He restrained a strong impulse to shoot as the grass finally parted and he could just see into the dark hole.

It was empty. He moved forward. Holding his tiny torch just above the ground and shading it with his hand, he made an inch by inch inspection. A human had squatted there recently, the shape was unmistakable and there were footprints. Then he saw a few grains of rice, wet, but not washed into the earth. It must have been dropped after the last downpour.

'Blast!' he swore softly, 'they're gone, and beckoning to Shamroz he moved forward a dozen yards until they came to the place where the Japs had crossed the embankment. An area six yards wide had been trampled flat, and judging by the footprints, several hundred men had crossed roughly four abreast and not long ago. What a target to miss, he thought as he searched around to discover the direction in which the enemy had gone.

Shamroz softly whistled up the patrol and they took up positions behind the embankment overlooking the road. No sooner had they settled down when an unearthly, but human, eerie wailing arose from the jungle opposite. In low mumbling tones it started, gradually became louder in volumn and intensity, then slowly died away to restart again with renewed vigour. It was a human voice of pain and anguish, and Vic came to the conclusion that it was a Jap who had fallen out of the march and was in his death throes, but he could not be sure. It might be a trap to tempt his patrol on to the road, which gave no cover.

He decided to wait. One party of Japs had gone but another might come, and he had not given up hope of carrying out a successful ambush. Indeed, the noise might well be a signal to an approaching enemy party.

It was almost midnight when the vigil started with a dozen pairs of eyes staring intently across the road to the dark gap in the jungle barely twenty paces distant. The wailing continued and kept nerves on edge, and now and then caused Vic's spine to prickle as the voice became more violent before dying away to a whisper and then silence for a few minutes. For an hour they bore it, and then a hand touched Vic, who jumped startled.

'Sahib,' whispered the Jemadar softly. 'Can I go across and kill him off?'

Vic would have given all the world to silence the voice but whispered, 'Sorry, Sahib, it might be a trap.' The Jemadar crept away disappointed. Lying in their wet clothes in the dripping grass on the sodden earth waiting for a chance to shoot and then get away quickly, and being compelled to listen to a death wail, was unpleasant.

Clouds scudded across the sky hiding the moon for periods of a few minutes, and during these, when visibility was down to a yard or so, the tension increased. The Japs would probably cross the road when darkness gave them cover. Supposing they have seen us and had gone around to attack from the rear? The thought flashed through Vic's mind, and he turned to peer into the darkness behind, his spine and neck prickly with apprehension and sweat creeping from his brow. He could see nothing and resumed his watch on the dark gap in the jungle across the road, hands on rifle.

An hour passed, but no movement came from the gap, and only the wailing voice which became weaker indicated a human presence.

Vic suddenly felt an insect on his right hand, an insect which seemed to have several legs, and a tail. It was on the back of his hand, moving around in a circle dragging its tail, and he was about to brush it off when it occurred to him that it might be a scorpion. He felt numb and wondered what to do. If he tried to knock it off, it might bite, which could be fatal. Better let it crawl. The thing began to move up his arm and he shuddered. Must get rid of it before it gets too far he thought. He very slowly moved his other arm to get the torch from his hip haversack, and brought it up gradually until he reckoned that it was within a few inches of the thing, whose progress was being hindered by the hairs on his forearm. He waited a second, jabbed hard and pressed the torch switch. He glimpsed a tangle of black legs as the scorpion was shot off into the grass and before it could recover, he squashed it under his torch.

Vic breathed his relief, wiped his arm and face and settled down again to wait, wondering anxiously for a moment whether scorpions lived in pairs, families or singly.

Another hour passed and it became too late for more Japs to cross the road so Vic decided to return to base. In a few moments, the patrol was heading north for camp, warmth, sleep, and perhaps something to drive out the wet. Trudging through the mud and water with far less care than before was refreshing after the vigil in the long grass. Inside the camp he quickly made his way to the command post, where Peter Reed, the duty officer, was waiting.

'The C.O. has warned Chris and Charlie Company to be ready to move out at first light,' he said.

'He will want artillery support. Both villages are out of range for our own guns, but those down the road will be able to reach the Japs. I think it would be better if Chris could get out five or six miles before first light,' Vic added.

After about four hours sleep, broken by Chris's visit during which the situation had been explained in detail, Vic was in the command post. The battalion was ready to move at a minute's notice. Chris had been on the wireless once, just before seven, reporting having found a couple of dead Japanese, and that he was about to enter the village of Thamigwe South. Half an hour passed and Vic sat waiting for more information, and getting visibly impatient.

'What the hell is happening?' he asked Peter, 'the C.O. will be hopping mad. Here he comes!'

Robin London was not mad, in fact he appeared quite the reverse.

'I wouldn't worry Chris yet. It's his first command in a scrap,' he said feelingly.

It was the C.O.'s too, and both Vic and Peter were fully aware of it and anxious that his first show should be a good one.

For two or three hours messages came through at frequent intervals. Chris and his company had searched Thamigwe South, killed half a dozen Japs and were patrolling towards Thamigwe North.

At eleven o'clock, he reported that he had seen the Jap in force and had exchanged fire.

Vic whispered to Peter, 'Tell the C.O. and alert all concerned. We shall be going out.'

He turned to the wireless, 'Hello Chris. Any idea of enemy strength?'

'Several hundred.'

'Have you any casualties?'

'One chest wound, Jemadar Mani Ram and several with flesh wounds.'

'Despatch wounded to milestone 125 where transport will collect them.'

The alert was sounded. Men emerged from huts and bivouacs at the double, scrambling into equipment as they ran. Those who had been asleep rubbed the tiredness from their eyes. They fell into sections and moved toward the road where every available vehicle stood nose to tail, with engines running.

'Can I come too?' a voice enquired from the mess. It belonged to Johnny Loosemore, a war correspondent who had arrived that morning. He was a genuine type and already popular.

'By all means, but grab a rifle! We may need your help,' said Vic grinning.

In less than ten minutes the two companies, each consisting of only two platoons and the small battalion headquarters had left the road and were making rapid progress across the flat and flooded countryside. The soldiers walked on the bunds, or banks, which bounded each small field, but heavy rain had made the tops of the bunds slippery and every now and again the soldiers slithered about for a moment and then splashed into the water. The sun was now at its height and beat down unmercifully on the eager, hurrying, sweating men and about their heads and in their wake a faint wispy haze of steam rose and lingered.

Presently, a rough track, fairly dry and running due east was located by the leading scouts and the men converged to take advantage of the easier going. The track ran almost straight to the most northern of the two villages which could now be clearly seen and soon a small group of men were spotted heading towards them. They were the wounded, and to Vic's amazement, Jemadar Mani Ram was among them.

'Salaam, Sahib!' he said with a grin, which was unusual, for Mani was a solemn dour type who seldom smiled or joked.

'I thought you were wounded?' queried Vic.

'That's right, Sahib. Here!' He bared his chest to display a small neat hole from which a narrow rivulet of thick blood had dribbled and congealed.

Just after the appointed time, the party met C Company, in positions six hundred yards from the occupied village.

At 14.15 hours orders were issued to advance. All went well for the first three hundred yards, and the supporting artillery opened fire. A hundred shells fell and normally some damage would have been done but they fell four hundred yards short of the target, kicking up numerous little spurts of water which were quite picturesque, but which provoked Vic to sudden anger.

'What the bloody hell are you doing?' he shouted over the wireless to the artillery officer. 'For heaven's sake, get another crump quick on the north edge of the village.'

The second batch of one hundred shells fell on the other side of the village causing no damage. As they fell, the Japs opened fire at a little under one hundred yards range and for ten minutes all hell was let loose. The leading troops dropped into the water. Those behind followed instantly, and the area where they lay was swept by a continuous storm of bullets. For a few minutes only the machine guns on the flank replied to the Jap fire, but soon the riflemen and light machine gunners wriggled through the water and started to shoot back. The noise increased as bullets exploded, zipped and whined in both directions.

Vic, lying behind cover, felt the thump of his heart and a sickening in his stomach. The battle was out of control. Disaster threatened. The advance had stopped. All the soldiers were pinned down by Japanese fire and could not move more than a yard backwards or forwards. There was only a hundred yards of no-man's land between the forward troops and the Japanese, who were well concealed in thick, almost bullet-proof bamboo. Only small momentary puffs of smoke from their weapons indicated their positions.

In the mad dash for cover, wireless communication had been interrupted but the operators soon settled themselves full length in the water with their sets on a bund. Vic tried to contact D Company, who were on the east flank and presumably out of danger, but there was no reply.

'Afraid there is no answer Sir, their set is out of action.'

The C.O. considered this for a few moments.

'There's only one thing to do. I'll go round to them with a few men and attack from the east. Get the artillery on the village but be ready to stop shelling in thirty minutes when I will attack. Advance then if you can, but use your own judgement.'

They checked watches, and the C.O. made off at a fast pace with his bodyguard toward the cover in the rear.

Keeping his head as low as possible, Vic examined the village through binoculars. His heart missed several beats as he saw the hundreds of Japs moving out towards both flanks, and, to his horror he realised that they were preparing to come out of the village in an encircling movement.

Taking the headphones, he spoke very deliberately to the artillery adjutant explaining the position, and adding, 'We are relying on you to get us out of trouble. Your last shell was four hundred yards short. Please correct.'

There was a pause of two or three minutes which, to Vic, lying looking through the glasses, seemed endless. The small arms fire was now spasmodic, with occasional bursts from the machine guns. His thoughts were broken by the two salvoes of shells which, with one exception, were on target.

As the Japs moved forward, slowly on both flanks, Vic asked for more artillery fire. 'Hell, what a mess,' he said to Johnny Loosemore, 'You certainly picked a good day to see some action.' The two men were lying a yard or so apart in the water which lapped around their shoulders. Vic looked over the top of the bund to observe the shells crashing in the village, and through his binoculars examined the front. The Japs on the flanks had gone to ground and those in the village were, for the time being, under cover, but the position was still tricky.

Vic considered the possibility of using artillery smoke to cover a withdrawal. He felt angry, depressed and frustrated, and wished that his available troops were double in number to enable him to attack. Then he considered attacking with his limited force and immediately rejected the idea. Time was short, only an hour of light remained and he was outnumbered by five or six to one and the Japs were in good defensive positions. His troops would be under fire from both flanks as well as the front. It would be suicide.

Instinctively he ducked quickly as a fusilade of bullets spat into the water within a few feet around him. He felt a sharp pain in his shoulder. The water began to turn red.

'Sahib, you are bleeding,' cried Shamroz, and Vic, feeling a little stupid, put his hand gingerly on his shoulder, and brought it away covered in blood. All sorts of horrible thoughts crossed his mind. Shamroz ripped a hole in the battledress and prodded gently, looking for the bullet.

'It's only a small wound, Sahib, but it's bleeding a lot.'

Vic helped Shamroz fix a field dressing, performing contortions to get the bandage round his body without exposing them both to fire. He was about to resume his position when the F.O.O. called him to the wireless.

Vic spoke impatiently into the mouthpiece, and then heard someone say:

'This is big No. 9 here. I want to speak to your No. 9.'

'Hells, bells, it's the general,' said Vic in an aside to his companion. Then into the wireless, 'He is not available. Can I take a message?'

'What is happening?' the general demanded.

Vic told him, and then was shaken rigid by the general's orders: 'I want you to attack at once.'

'I regret that an attack is not possible without very heavy casualties. We intend to withdraw from the present position leaving a force to keep contact and to resume operations at first light,' Vic replied quietly.

The general became nettled. 'I expect you to attack tonight. Will you please pass the order to your C.O. at once.'

Vic swore to himself, but he replied, 'Wireless communications between us and our C.O.'s party do not exist. If we stay in our present position we shall be attacked in force. Any attack we may mount must be from a different position.'

'Right. I expect you to attack if at all possible.'

Vic turned away from the wireless fuming, his indignation rising. 'How the hell does he expect me to attack?' he exploded to himself. Angry and bitter, he resumed his position in the water, and made a new appreciation of the position, but it added up to the same thing as before, except that now the general was demanding an attack.

The forward troops were pinned down at short range, the C.O. and D Company were in trouble and out of touch, the Japs were becoming more menacing, and time was getting short.

In the race to Rangoon, it had been right and necessary to attack and push on, but now the situation was different. The Japs were in a bad way and intent only on getting across the Sittang. Physically unfit, they were suffering badly from foot rot, malnutrition, fever and jungle sores, and were desperately short of food and ammunition. They had already endured incredible hardships and suffering and the survivors, in desperation, would fight like rats to reach safety. But why risk our lives unnecessarily? Let's kill them off by all means, but for heaven's sake, let us do it sensibly! Find them, cut off their escape, and then bring down the artillery, and not attack across flat open country, exposing our troops without reason.

'It's bloody silly,' he concluded aloud, 'and I'm going to get out of here as soon as possible.' The rain started. A few big drops, and then the heavens opened in typically monsoon manner, reducing visibility to fifty yards almost instantaneously.

The storm hit his face with tremendous force as he stood up.

He looked toward the enemy positions, now shrouded behind a wall of driving rain which swept across the fields soaking friend and foe alike. As his eyes searched for movement, the rain fell off his battered bush hat in a steady stream. The cold water soaked through the field-dressing and his wound tingled.

Attack, attack, attack. The words kept running through his mind, jarring, irritating, but not now causing indignation. The rain had come to his aid and, general or no general, he was going to withdraw. He suddenly felt happy.

'Put thirty smoke shells three hundred yards short of the village, lift one hundred yards and repeat,' he said briskly to the artillery officer. He gave orders to C and A Companies, the former to pull back as soon as the smoke thickened and the latter to provide covering fire. Within twenty five minutes, the operation was complete. All troops were four hundred yards or more away from the village, and Vic felt pleased and relieved. He knew his decision had been right, and the possibility of the general being angry did not worry him at all. The men had been saved from a difficult position and lived to fight again. A small procession of men struggling hard against the wind and rain appeared. It was the C.O.'s party.'

'D Company have two killed and nine or ten badly wounded,' Robin gasped.

Vic shuddered involuntarily. 'Christ,' he said.

'Twenty men of D Company are too close to the Jap to break off contact,' Robin said. He continued, 'I've given orders for a platoon to stand by to watch the Jap and to get the twenty men out of trouble after dark. Now let's get the wounded back to base quickly before we meet another party of Japs.'

Vic made his report, including the general's order. 'I'm afraid, Sir, I've let you in for a lot of trouble,' he concluded apologetically.

'Don't worry about it, Vic, I'm very glad you got the men back without casualties.'

Darkness had fallen before the march began with Vic leading and the C.O. with the stretcher party bringing up the rear. Caution was necessary for somewhere in the distance ahead, were several thousand Japanese, advancing toward them. For Vic, avoidance was the order of the night. The ground was slippery after the rain and the men slipped and fell now and again as they made their way over the uneven surface in the dark. The six miles to the road took almost four hours, and it was after ten o'clock when they heard the sound of transport and saw headlights. In camp, a hot meal and dry clothes were ready.

The C.O. and Vic made a tour of the lines before entering the Mess where the C.O. handed Vic a mug of rum laced with tea. 'Here you are, drink this.'

Vic gulped the mixture quickly.

'What a bloody day, and worse to come tomorrow!'

But the morrow was not too bad. The general arrived without warning although he had been half-expected, and after conferring with the C.O. he appeared to be friendly disposed to all, including Vic, who had a chip on his shoulder about attacks, not to mention a six inch gash where a bullet had entered and apparently come out again.

13

A FEW ESCAPE

Under cover of darkness and very heavy rain, the Japs in Thamigwe North eluded the watching patrol, and moved to Payala, where another Sikh platoon discovered to their joy and amazement that the Japs were not taking any precautions. They were, in fact, moving about in the village quite freely. The patrol leader wirelessed to Vic. 'We've found them at Payala, they haven't seen us yet, they are a sitting target for artillery.'

Mike Cooper, the 493 Battery commander had already given warning orders to his gunners to lay on Payala. Mike asked for the number of shells required.

'As many as possible in as short a time as possible,' Vic replied.

Fortunately, Payala had previously been registered by the artillery and this procedure which had been so tedious on the previous day, was not now necessary. From out of the blue, hundreds of shells would explode on the Japs without warning and with devastating effect as they walked or lay about in the village unprotected and defenceless against the fury of high explosive by the ton. None of our own troops would be exposed to fire: they were only required to wait for the Japs to run into their small arms fire.

From down the road more 25-pounders and the medium heavies stirred and rumbled. Instinctively, the Japs ran for the open spaces and safety, but they were mistaken. The Sikhs caught them in a net, criss-crossed with vicious rifle and machine gun fire. Japs fell by the score, dead, or to die in the mud and water. The Sikhs halted them, and bewildered, like hunted rabbits, the enemy went to ground.

Fed by sweating gunners stripped to the waist, their tanned

bodies glistening in the rain, the guns spat shell after shell, and the Japs, caught between two fires dashed frantically back into the village. The gunner officer O.P. now overhead in a light aircraft, reported their return and everybody waited impatiently until the stragglers were within the confines of Payala. New orders went down the lines: barrels moved gently, almost imperceptibly as the guns returned to their original range. There was a split second pause, the guns shuddered and the storm, thick and fast, of screaming shells tore through the heavy atmosphere.

The Japs, hungry, harassed and humiliated, had neither mental nor physical defence and as the shells exploded, they ran blindly for the open fields. To the north, south, east and west they scattered without sense of direction. A running, stumbling, rabble of soldiers, instinct their only guide, and for the moment they were safe, for on recovering, they fled east in ones, twos and threes without forming a target for the voracious guns.

Another patrol found them in a village halted for the night to lick their wounds, the medium heavy artillery took their toll and the enemy were driven to seek safety in the flooded paddy fields, leaving behind their dead and dying.

The survivors shambled, resolute and with amazing willpower, towards the Sittang, where a new hazard awaited them for here the guerillas harried and harassed them for days, but somehow at least a hundrd Japs managed to find or build boats or rafts and escape across the mile-wide flooded river to the haven of the foothills on its eastern banks.

During the late afternoon of 2 July, the leg weary patrol made its way back to Nyaungbintha, having completed the job of seeing the Japs off the premises. The first battle of the breakout was over.

Johnny Loosemore's article in S.E.A.C. newspaper was pleasant to read if perhaps a little overdone. It read:

PUNJABIS BREAK JAP RIVER ESCAPE BID

'2 July (delayed) – After a severe mauling at the hands of a battalion of the 15th Punjab Regiment and field and medium guns of the Royal Artillery, 200 Japanese – remnants of a formation which crossed the Rangoon-Mandalay Road several days ago 800 strong are today fighting their way through a swarm of guerillas in an attempt to reach the

> Sittang River, writes an Indian Army observer.
>
> On 30 June they were heavily attacked in Thamigwe village by the 15th Punjabs, and were so badly mauled they pulled out under cover of darkness.
>
> Next morning a patrol of the Punjabs found them in the village of Payalaha, a mile and a half nearer the Sittang.
>
> Directed by an Air O.P. the R.A. field and medium guns opened up on them.
>
> Disorganised by the heavy fire, the Japs fled across the open paddy with shells landing amongst them.
>
> 600 JAPS KILLED
>
> By this morning the scattered remnants had concentrated further to the east. Once again, patrols found them, the artillery shelled them, and they scattered into the jungle.
>
> Latest reports are that guerillas are between them and the river, and a running fight is on.
>
> An A.P.I. war correspondent reports that the Punjabs killed 600 out of the formation of 800 Japanese who made a co-ordinated effort to cross the Eastern line.
>
> On the Mawchi road flooded chaungs and waist-deep mud hamper operations.
>
> Today's S.E. Asia Command communique from Kandy says the Japanese have launched a series of small scale attacks on our positions in the area of the bend of the Sittang River, 25 miles east N.E. of Pegu. Fighting is continuing.
>
> Japanese who crossed the Pegu Sittang river 26 miles N.E. of Pegu entered the village of LE-INZU, where fighting is also in progress.'

This was of course only half the story, and an inquest on the battle was held immediately.

Whilst the battalion had achieved a measure of success, the battle could have been much more successful. Several things had not worked out as well as they might have done. In the first place, the enemy, in strength, had been allowed to get within a mile or so of the road undetected, and the subsequent ambush patrol had been too late. Time had been wasted in mounting the attack on Thamigwe, due to the artillery registration and the breakdown in wireless communication. On the other hand, once the Japs had moved from Thamigwe, the patrolling had been most efficient, and the use of artillery most effective. The combined results had been satisfactory but not good enough.

The first round in the battle of the breakout had been won, but only on points, which perhaps was inevitable for new techniques and tactics were necessary to meet an unusual and unique situation and these had not been sufficiently developed.

It was not easy to have a third of the depleted battalion on patrol all the time indefinitely and, unfortunately, there was no major enemy breakout for almost three weeks, during which the monsoon made the conditions even more arduous and exhausting. Every day and night heavy rain fell for long periods, and when it stopped, out came the sun for an hour or so, very hot and almost unbearable to men on patrol who trudged distances of up to twenty miles, often through water knee-deep every two or three days.

In such circumstances, it became somewhat difficult to keep soldiers always alert and constantly on their toes, and when there were signs of weariness the C.O. ordered a fifteen minute foot drill to be carried out every three days. This had the desired effect, and the men appeared to enjoy their session of square bashing, due no doubt to the feeling of wellbeing it provoked.

A few prisoners were captured in a very poor state of health on the jungle tracks. The first a private soldier, was in a pitiful state, and gave the impression of being quite glad to die. Thin, with his flesh drawn very tight, and covered with angry suppurating sores, he shivered and perspired simultaneously, obviously stricken with malaria. His face bore a strange expression, resigned, composed and peaceful, like the face of a dead man.

He maintained an absolute silence until a medical orderly attempted to remove his socks, when he came to life and let loose a prolonged burst of angry protestation. With very feeble gestures of his hands he protected his feet, and then proceeded to demonstrate his reason. Quite unperturbed, slowly, and with great deliberation, he rolled down his right sock, his eyes intent on his foot until the leg portion of the sock was neatly rolled. He then looked up into the faces of the doctor, Vic, and the medical orderly. He paused and resumed taking off his sock.

As he started to peel off the foot of the sock the flesh came with it. The sock had become an integral part of his foot, flesh and wool were together in one piece. The onlookers averted their eyes: the Jap still quite composed, pulled his sock on again, gently, and very slowly.

He was given food, a cigarette, some medical attention, and removed to sit outside the command post against a tree.

A gunner officer who, before the war, had lived in Japan and spoke fluent Japanese, came to have a few words with the prisoner. By the oddest coincidence they knew each other. In peacetime, the prisoner had been a coalman, and had delivered coal to the officer's house! The prisoner broke into a torrent of words and feeble gsticulations, and when, after a few moments, he became silent and looked sad, despair was written all over his face. He said nothing new, or of interest to the battalion, and he departed to division H.Q. carrying his boots and hobbling painfully to the truck.

'Poor blighter, he is in a bad way,' said Vic.

'My God, yes,' replied the Doctor, 'he should have died long ago. I've never seen foot-rot like that before, it was horrible. If they are all like that, this campaign won't last long.'

'They are not all as bad Doc. Those C Company killed at Thamigwe were tough, big and apparently well fed.'

'By the way, Tina has invited you to her house for a meal,' the Doctor said, almost as an after thought.

'Who the hell is Tina?' Vic demanded.

'You know, the interpreter,' the doctor replied in a confident voice.

'Is that her name?'

'Not really, it's unpronounceable, but it starts with a T, so I call her Tina.'

'And how friendly are you with this Tina?' Vic enquired suspiciously.

'Oh, not in the way you think,' the doctor gestured smiling a little.

'How the devil do you know how I think?' Vic asked.

'Well, you know Vic, you are a good friend of mine,' the doctor said, adding very hastily, 'there's nothing going on between us if that is what you think.'

'I should think not indeed. When do we go to her house?'

'Tomorrow night at eight o'clock.'

'Doc, are you out of your mind? Eight o'clock! Long after

dark,' Vic demanded.

'Well, I thought – ' the doctor began weakly, thought better of it and stopped in mid-sentence.

'I think we ought to forget the whole thing for the time being.'

'I take it there is no harm in going to Pyu during daylight!' the Doc asked with a touch of sarcasm in his voice.

'It could be arranged, subject, of course, to Jap activity.'

'All right, I'll tell Tina we decline the invitation,' the doctor said in a wooden voice.

'No, say you will let her know in a day or so.'

That evening, a Sikh patrol braved the hazards of entering Nyaungbintha after dark. They negotiated the many trip wires and booby traps across the approach tracks, and risked being killed by their own comrades. It took them almost an hour to travel the final furlong and get within calling distance of the sentries, who fortunately, recognised their voices and admitted them immediately.

The four Sikhs were soaking wet and their beards glistened with raindrops. They were not due to return from patrol, but had brought in a prisoner of war, the first Japanese commissioned officer to be captured. He was at once escorted to the command post where Vic interrogated him. He was young, not more than twenty five, arrogant and sullen. He spoke English but refused to converse other than to give his name. He refused food and a cigarette. He had no weapon, and in his pockets were found an empty expensive cigarette case, an obscene photograph and an equally obscene pen and ink sketch.

He was put under guard for the night, and Vic returned to his bivouac just after midnight. Five hours later the jemadar adjutant awakened him.

'It's the prisoner, Sahib. He wants the guard to shoot him. He has been awake all night, begging the sentries to kill him. They are going crazy. What shall we do?'

'If he makes a noise stick something in his mouth and gag him. I'll see him at 0800 hours, and now Sahib, I'm going to sleep again.'

The enemy continued to show a great interest in Nyaungbintha, and for three nights in succession Jap patrols of half a dozen men fired indiscriminately into the position. They did no harm except to the nerves, for everybody, having expected an attack for so long, was in a state of tension, at first not to any serious extent, but sufficient to assume that when the bullets whined overhead, a fanatical attack was imminent. The fall of the position would have been disastrous, for a good and safe route would become available to the Jap, who could then hold Nyaungbintha while their 28th Army escaped to the east.

The mere thought of such a possibility was enough to cause officers of the Punjabis sleepless nights and nightmares, and provoke symptoms not unlike those of malaria, when the body alternatively boils and freezes.

The threat of a mass attack was very real, and while all inside Nyaungbintha were very confident, experienced and courageous, an enemy force of perhaps two thousand, or even one thousand, charging in their fanatical manner with complete disregard for life, could cause havoc and perhaps neutralise the position by sheer weight of numbers. A night attack was more likely and there was some justification for the tension, for the thumping of hearts, and for the prickly shivers which ran up and down spines when a fusilade of bullets swept the position. This is it, everyone thought, and felt very stupid an hour later when dead silence prevailed again.

Vic accepted an invitation from the commanding officer of the Burmese battalion of the People's Army to attend a conference at Pyu, and with the connivance of the doctor, decided to combine business with pleasure and accept, at the same time, the long standing invitation to a meal at Tina's house, which was just across the road from the H.Q. of the Burmese battalion.

He felt a strong feeling of foreboding and reluctance to visit their H.Q. They had, until recently, fought with the Japanese against the British, and they had not displayed any clear evidence of the direction in which their loyalties lay.

Vic felt rather like Daniel walking into the lion's den, so he took unusual precautions. His driver and Shamroz were briefed as bodyguards. He tucked a loaded pistol under his armpit, and put a couple of primed grenades in his pockets, and then drove to the People's Army H.Q. Here he was greeted cordially and conducted to the conference room which was in a large wooden building tucked away in a side street. There was a huge heavy table in the centre of the room, and around the walls were hung several large photographs of men whom he did not recognise, except two of Stalin which were in the most prominent positions and flanked by draped flags. Vic wondered where the flags and photographs came from, and where they had been during the Jap occupation. He did not appreciate the significance of the decorations, so he pretended not to notice.

At the back of his mind there lurked the feeling that there was something wrong. His fingers strayed to the grenades and pistol, and he felt reassured. Duty compelled him to face the situation, and he endeavoured, with some measure of success, or so it seemed at the time, to obtain some assistance from the Burmese battalion. During the past few weeks they had expended a great deal of ammunition without any results, and it was now necessary to get results with less ammunition. This, the commanding officer promised to do.

The conference over, Vic walked across the road to join the doctor at Tina's house where he was most cordially received by Tina and her mother, a Burmese lady of about sixty years. They sat on cushions on the floor, and ate from a table a foot high, which was overladen with countless dishes of food. Later Doc told Vic that there were in fact twenty seven different varieties, but as Vic surveyed the food he only recognised curried eggs, prawns and chicken, with their usual subsidiary dishes.

During the Japanese occupation Tina had been interned in the camp at Toungoo, which had been destroyed by the Allies on their advance to Rangoon, and she recounted some of her experiences.

It was not a pleasant topic, but Tina, well educated and sophisticated, obviously welcomed the opportunity for conversation in English which she spoke perfectly and without a trace of accent. As the meal drew to a close they talked of other things, of after the war, of before the war, of Tina's father, an American teak grower, and of her hopes and aspirations. Above all, she said frankly and without trace of shyness, she intended to marry an Englishman, preferably an officer, and have a large family. She looked at Vic who felt the time had come to go. The doctor was in an impish mood, which Vic found somewhat disconcerting.

Neither had seen a woman since the previous Christmas and then only from a distance. They were being entertained by a most attractive and charming girl who looked upon them mistakenly, but with absolute certainty, as her rescuers from the horrors of internment. In her company they felt relaxed, refreshed, and pervaded with a sense of well-being.

Vic was anxious to be off, away from Tina. She was young and her eyes held an invitation, warm and unmistakable. Here was grace and beauty and the fluttering of eyes, the suppleness of youth and the promise of pleasure, pure and good, and complete escape, if only for a short time. They had eaten well and the visit had been a tonic. Vic rose to go, and thanked her.

'But please come again any time, by yourself or with the doctor,' Tina said. 'We will be very happy to see you.' She spoke quietly, with sincerity.

'We would like to, but there is work to be done and it is difficult to take an hour off but we will try, and in any case, the doctor will be coming to see the sick,' Vic said.

The two officers walked outside to where Shamroz and the driver sat in the front seat of the Jeep. In the back seat two Japanese soldiers sat still. On seeing the officers approach, the four hurriedly scrambled out.

'We report the capture of two prisoners of war,' Shamroz said solemnly, throwing a smart salute.

'Where?' asked Vic.

'Here,' replied Shamroz.

'How?' asked Vic.

'The Burmese battalion had them.'

'O.K. Put them in the back and look after them. I'll drive,' Vic replied.

The afternoon had been a pleasant escape, a relief from mud, rain and the Japs. Later, in the mess, both the doctor and Vic were in fine form and enjoyed the gentle leg-pulling from envious brother officers. It was easy to parry the sly dig and to disarm the over inquisitive, the doctor in the crackly hesitant voice stopped all wise-cracks.

'Call yourselves officers?' he demanded, his eyes twinkling.

'Why, I don't believe you have any idea of fighting. You talk like children when you bring in one, just one, poor miserable prisoner after risking your necks and goodness knows how many of your men. On the other hand, Vic and I do the job in style. We have an excellent lunch with a very charming girl, and without going to any trouble at all, we bring back two able-bodied prisoners.'

'Well said,' Vic rejoined, 'now let's get down to some serious poker.'

14

MASSACRE

Brian Rogers had rejoined the battalion on 17 July. Robin London, the C.O. received news of his father's death and departed suddenly on compassionate leave. John Smythe unexpectedly found himself in command, and not without a little apprehension, he assumed control of the five hundred Hindus, Muslims, Sikhs, and the Christian officers who, tough and skilful, prepared in an atmosphere of mounting tension to do battle.

There was every indication that the Japanese 28th Army would attempt to escape before the end of the month and that some elements at least would attempt to contain Nyaungbintha and its derelict railway station from which the enemy could control a mile of road and jungle and allow a force, several thousand strong, to escape quickly and safely.

The monsoon would continue and the rain would fall, most of the time, day in and day out. The Nips would fight like cornered rats, desperate and vicious. Had they not fought like that at Thamigwe on 28 June, the men asked themselves and one another. Since then, two more battalions had been hurriedly moved into the 6th Punjabi's sector. It was clear that Divisional Headquarters were now of the opinion that the enemy 'breakout' in the area would be on a more intensive scale than they had thought at first. Additional troops reduced the 6th Punjabi's area to a width of about six miles, and to everybody's delight, the unit at Kanyutkwin was their own 1st Battalion. If any spur to fight well had been needed in the 6th, none better than the arrival of their senior battalion could be possible. The two units now stood side by side on the road ready to stop the enemy onslaught, each determined to emulate the other.

The original area now held by three battalions was commanded by Brigadier Flewitt D.S.O., and quite naturally the force became simply 'Flewforce'. On arrival at Nyaungbintha he had set up a skeleton H.Q., put himself in the picture, made a few quiet but very pointed remarks and expressed his satisfaction.

Scholarly in appearance, he was soon regarded as a friend. He listened quietly to John's apprciation and agreed that the killing ground should be on the east of the road because here the country was open, offered little cover except in the villages, and was where the enemy was most likely to be found.

The Jap had hitherto only moved across the road by night and there was no reason to expect a change in his tactics, and, since they could only cover about nine miles under cover of darkness in one night, it was reasonable to assume that at first light those who crossed the road would be found on a line running north and south roughly four and a half miles from the road. Villages on this line were being patrolled at dawn and most were being occupied by night.

John decided to concentrate the battalion on Nyaungbintha, with the exception of small patrols, with the object of having all his available troops immediately at hand to meet the expected Jap attack or their attempt to escape. The decision was given to Vic, his adjutant, while they dressed just before dawn.

These two still shared a bivouac consisting of a large tarpaulin tied to tree branches at one end, supported at a lower height at the other end by wooden poles, and supported and pegged down at the sides, except for a loose flap which formed the door. It had been cunningly devised by their orderlies and made into a spacious room by current standards, and provided a degree of privacy which was something of a luxury.

It had one serious drawback - it was very exposed and within forty paces of the perimeter wire. Night after night John and Vic had lain on their wooden beds when bullets were flying, speculating on the chances of being hit. After several long and quite serious discussions, they had decided that the chances were slight, but as a precaution, they carefully arranged that the transport should be parked around the bivouac. This operation took a few days to organise, for it was necessary to avoid any sign of fright on the part of the C.O. and the adjutant.

Each had confessed to the other their fear of being killed while asleep; both had admitted to being scared to death of the

Japanese getting into the positions during darkness and finding their way into the bivouac with grenades.

'It's all right for you Vic,' John had said. 'You are away from the door.'

'But I'm nearer to the perimeter,' protested Vic. 'I'm sure to get hit first.'

'Oh well, if our number is up, we shall get it anyway. It's no good worrying,' John had replied.

The night of 19 July had been quiet, even the rain had ceased and the moon had lit up the interior of the bivouac and in its light the two officers had slept peacefully, like children.

As Vic rolled out of bed he sang a few bars of 'Ilkley Moor bah t'at', or what passed to him as singing for he had no ear for a tune.

'Don't you know any other bloody song?' grumbled John.

'Every bloody morning you get out of bed to sing that one, flat as hell.'

Vic looked up in amazement. 'Sorry, wasn't aware I was singing.'

During the morning, patrol reports were negative, and John decided to pay a combined business and pleasure call on the 1st Battalion at Kanyatkwin, five miles to the south. He left at about 1130 hours and intended to return at 1400 hours, but the enemy had other ideas, and at 1300 hours they had established a medium machine gun position on the main road four hundred yards south of Nyaungbintha.

It happened so suddenly that no one had time to feel the customary jitters. Lunch had just ended. Vic and Peter were in the command post plotting patrol routes when the gun opened fire. Bullets whined overhead as the ominous rat-tat-tat continued for a few seconds, paused, and started again.

'Hells bells, this is it,' Vic exclaimed and rushed outside.

'Down there, Sahib,' a sentry called pointing down the road, and sure enough, 'down there' was a little bunch of men, only their heads visible like shadowy Charlie Chad's over a grass bank. In a second or two Frontier Force machine guns were firing back; a bugle sounding the Stand To joined in the din, men rushed to positions on the perimeter, and messages were phoned north and south along the road to stop the traffic.

Major Ghulam Mohd, O.C. of the Mobile Company reported to the command post and then joined Peter and Vic behind a thick tree. They stood for a minute without comment, their eyes searching the edge of the jungle for movement. Each thought that this was the anticipated attack and watched anxiously expecting hordes of Japs to charge across the road. The Sikhs, whose defences were partially on the other side of the road, waited quietly in their dug outs for the anticipated fanatical charge. Just as suddenly as it started, the Jap fire ceased, the heads disappeared, and the officers returned to the command post.

'Looks like a storm in a tea cup but we must make sure. Will you go around to their rear and sweep back through to A Company?' Vic said to Ghulam.

Vic sat down to await Ghulam's first report which came through in ten minutes.

'The Japs have gone back into the jungle. We are now searching.'

The telephone bell rang. 'Hello Vic. John here. What the hell is going on? We got a message stopping all traffic and we heard some firing. What is happening?' He sounded agitated and obviously worried. Vic couldn't resist pulling his leg.

'The ruddy Jap got across the road four hundred yards south of here and until they are shifted or withdraw, we can't allow any traffic through.'

'How many are there?' John asked.

'Oh, I should say about a thousand,' Vic replied lightly.

'Christ,' John swore, then tumbled to it. 'You so and so. What is the real story?'

Vic gave him the details, assuring him that everything was under control.

The mobile company finished their search without finding the Japs and the battalion stood down, very much on their toes. The C.O. returned quite convinced that the main Japanese breakout would start that night, and immediately called an officers' conference. When the details had been completed, and all questions answered, John spoke in his quiet cultured voice. He was a little hesitant at first but quickly gained confidence.

'There are twenty to thirty thousand Japanese soldiers within ten miles of this place, preparing to move, or actually moving in this direction. A fair number might be coming to attack our position. Such an attack would obviously be the prelude to a mass breakout, and therefore if the attack does not materialise before the Japs start to cross the road, we can assume that we won't be attacked, except perhaps for diversionary purposes. I believe that we shall have Japs all over the countryside in a day or so and speed in destroying them will be of vital importance.

I do not want any set piece attacks. For one thing, there won't be time, and secondly, I don't wish to incur unnecessary casualties. We've got the finest artillery in the world, and the Japs, even when in the villages, will be sitting targets provided they are held in one position long enough. They won't be able to dig in. We must find them quickly, cut off their escape, and shell them hard and quick.

If the Japs move as I think they will, it won't be a question of merely finding a party of them, say fifty or sixty, and dealing with them in a day, as we have been accustomed to. There will possibly be several parties requiring attention every morning. They will be located and liquidated with the utmost speed.

It's possible that we won't get much sleep during the next few days but in ten days or so, it will be all over.'

He paused and looked around before he spoke again. 'I shall have to ask for the impossible; you will have to ask for the impossible, we will all get it, as indeed we have got it on many occasions in the past.'

There was nothing more to be said. Several officers stayed to play poker and the early evening passed pleasantly except for two rifle shots close to the perimeter. The light flickered and the window shutters rattled. Everybody became quite still and silent for perhaps a second. Nothing more happened, and without comment, the game was resumed.

Away to the west, six men, an N.C.O. and five sepoys lay on the wet ground and, hidden by the thick undergrowth, watched and listened. They could hear the murmuring of the river as it flowed swiftly past, and the incessant dripping of rain from trees and bushes. The rain fell hard for short periods, and now and then there was the startling call of a bird, piercing the quiet of the night. Close at hand there was the frequent strange and unexplained rustle in the grass and low undergrowth. Frequently, after a storm, the heavy curtain of cloud parted for a moment or so, sometimes for as long as five minutes, and the moon, almost in its full glory, lit the scene with a ghostly brilliance. Then the watchers stirred and adjusted their positions to get a better view.

The watchers were on the extreme edge of the jungle and between them and the river was a patch of flat grass which dipped gently at the ford where a single bushy topped tree sheltered a small derelict wooden shed. Here the surface of the water rippled and swirled before becoming more sedate in the deep water beyond. The far bank had been long submerged and the water overflowed, and lapped quietly forward and backward, on the gentle grassy slope. The water ended eighty yards short of trees, growing on a confusion of small hills beyond. A narrow track ran from the river and disappeared into the trees. Behind the small hills there was a black mass of high ground which towered into the clouds, dark, dense, and full of mystery. Within its dark depths, the Japs were hidden.

In the mess, the poker school had dwindled until only John, Brian, Vic and the doctor remained. They seemed strangely reluctant to go to bed, and the game dragged on for an hour later than usual, but interest was flagging and the poker gradually became only a pretence. The doctor chuckled happily as he totted up the score. 'I seem to have had a good evening,' he said, a note of apology in his voice.

'What do you mean, a good evening,' Brian demanded. 'You always have a good evening, you're the biggest card sharper I've ever met.'

The doctor laughed heartily. 'Why that's nonsense, Vic has won, too! You can't bluff, that's your trouble, isn't it Vic?'

'I couldn't agree more, but I'm tired. Who's for bed?' and Vic yawned as he stood up.

'Not you,' a quiet voice came from behind, startling the four officers.

It was Peter Reed, wearing soft shoes, who had entered the room unseen and unheard.

'Sorry to butt in, but I've got a patrol leader on the wireless.' It was the Havildar at Gyobin.

'We haven't seen anything, but there is a lot of noise coming from the trees, Japs are moving north along the foothills,' the patrol leader reported.

'Message received, well done. How long did the noise last and have you any idea of the number of enemy?' Vic asked.

'About ten minutes, and there is still some noise now. I

believe the party must be two or three hundred strong.'

'O.K. report again in ten minutes.'

'Wilco. Out.'

Vic picked up the telephone. 'Get the Ford patrol quickly.' There was a short buzz and a low voice said, 'Who is that?' Passwords were exchanged and the warning given that the enemy were approaching the ford.

'They may cross the ford. Report their direction as soon as possible,' Vic ordered.

John, the C.O. decided to wait to see what happened, and he and Vic discussed the situation.

'If they don't cross the Kun Chaung at the ford, presumably they will cross higher up and then follow the line of the Zaha Chaung to the road,' John said.

'That is logical, but it will take several hours and they won't reach the road until at least five o'clock. Something must have gone wrong in their timing. It looks as if we will find them in the area of Zaha and Sindegon at breakfast time.'

In a few minutes, orders had been given for the Jat Company to occupy Zaha and for the Sikhs to take up the trail at the ford. A further telephone call to the patrol at the ford revealed that the enemy were still moving north and had made no attempt to cross the Kun Chaung.

'In that case we may as well get a few hours sleep. The Jap won't be crossing the road until about five o'clock,' remarked John.

'They are not very intelligent, unless, of course, their movement is a feint. If we had been in their position, we would have moved up to the Kun Chaung during daylight, and moved like hell across the road as soon as it became dark,' rejoined Vic.

'I don't get it at all. We'll have to be very careful in the morning,' John replied.

The Jap Company had barely taken up their position in and around Zaha before the darkness lifted and the grey dawn crept quickly across the flooded paddy fields. With it came the Japs.

To facilitate their movement across strange flooded country, they straggled close together in threes and fours, and the noise they made was heard a good half a mile away. Their time of arrival in the area was unfortunate; their method of movement most unwise, for had they been thirty minutes earlier and deployed after crossing the road, and then moved quietly, most of them would have lived. Their mistake in underestimating the enemy was the type of error or misjudgement that is only made once in war.

There were two columns, each about one hundred strong and heading, presumably, for Zaha and Leikpaw. They marched on parallel lines, two furlongs apart.

C Company wirelessed news of their approach a few minutes before 0500 hours. The 25-pounder guns prepared for action. Ghulam, the company commander, gave a minute by minute progress report on the enemy movement to Vic, who sat beside Mike Cooper, the artillery battery commander in the tiny command post.

Vic looked at Mike. 'Bit awkward having two targets, isn't it?' he queried.

'We can cope. We have registered on Zaha. I've laid four guns on each target.'

Vic's fingers drummed on the table as he waited and he smiled as he thought of the Japs moving unsuspecting into the artillery fire. John, who had left the command post twenty minutes earlier, returned.

'What are you waiting for?' he asked quietly.

'The Japs are slow. Here's Ghulam again.'

'Enemy are on target area. Fire now!' Ghulam shouted.

'O.K. Mike, fire now!' Vic shouted. Instantly the guns boomed.

The guns fired again and again on the defenceless enemy, who lay in the open paddy fields. After about fifty percent of their force had been killed and wounded, the rest scattered and made their way in ones and twos around the flanks to the village of Sindagon. Here they were given a few minutes to concentrate and then the shelling was resumed. Immediately, they ran in all directions. Many were killed by machine gun fire, but a number who ran toward the east, escaped. No chase ensued for other more important targets were now demanding attention.

The Sikhs, who had moved west just before dawn, soon made contact with the enemy and proceeded to shell and prod them on their way. By midday, a stream of Japs were crossing the road. They poured over the railway embankment by the hundred, in columns eighty and one hundred yards long. They moved into Akyat and Kon-in. A few minutes elapsed while they concentrated and then the guns opened fire, raking the targets from end to end with tons of high explosive.

A quarter of a mile to the east of the villages, a platoon of Punjabis with two medium machine guns waited for the Japs to run, and their wait was not in vain. Parties of enemy ran from the proverbial frying pan into the fire and perished in the flooded fields by the score. The shelling continued until the light failed. The guns at Nyaungbintha had been firing on and off since dawn, and at times, the medium heavies at Kanyutkwin had made a substantial contribution. With the darkness came peace and quiet.

'Come along you two, we need a drink,' John said to Vic and Mike, adding, 'It's been a good day. How many bodies have been counted?'

'Seventy in the Zaha area and forty eight in Leikpaw, but there's been no time to count in other areas. At a conservative estimate I would put the number killed at two hundred plus, and there were two prisoners brought in from Zibyugin.'

'We are a bit thin on the perimeter at the moment. It would be a little unfortunate if the Japs attacked now,' John remarked.

'Oh, I wouldn't say that. The Jats are now holding the fort, and in their present mood would keep an enemy division at bay. They certainly returned from Zaha with their tails up.' Vic replied.

'Yes, there is nothing like success to raise morale,' said John, rising from his chair.

A few minutes later Vic entered their bivouac where his C.O. was taking a bath. John sat in a saucer-shaped canvas which, supported around the edges by short pieces of wood, six inches high, contained a pool of water two feet in diameter. John's very pink body overflowed as he lathered himself vigorously; the bivouac smelt strongly of Dettol. Having completed his soaping, John reached for the pint-sized mug. With the soap suds running down into his eyes, he missed the mug, and Vic walked over and put it into his hand.

'Thanks,' John grunted obviously deep in thought, and started the rinsing process. Beside his bath stood a four-gallon petrol can full of cold water, and this John dipped out with the mug to sluice the lather off. He gasped as the cold water made its first impact and spluttered when it ran down over his face and into his eyes and mouth. Water splashed on the floor outside the bath, and Vic, lying full length on his bed in his corner of the bivouac, watched the operation with amusement. John stood up, grabbed a towel and dried himself with considerable vigour.

'That's better. Aren't you going to bath?' he demanded of Vic.

'Yes, of course, presently. There's only room for one at a time,' Vic replied, adding hastily, 'Hey! Steady on, you're choking me!'

John was smothering his body with talcum powder and for a few moments he was completely hidden from Vic's view by the powder which filled the confined space like a thick fog. When it cleared and John's pink body reappeared, Vic enquired, 'How many tins of talcum do you use in a week?'

'About two or three. Can't do without the stuff. I start sweating like a pig at dawn, and continue all day. I get sore as hell all over if I don't use it and my so and so piles have been painful during the past few days. Must get them cut or something before long,' John said feelingly.

'What you need, and all of us for that matter, is a fortnight in Darjeeling where the nights are cool and the days are dry and warm,' Vic said.

'It's bloody well raining there too,' John grumbled. 'I'm now going to ring up the First Battalion, and pull their legs. See you in the mess.' He went out, and popped his head in again.

'How many Japs can I say we killed?' he asked.

'About six hundred and fifty. Its not true of course, but it should keep them quiet for a day or so,' adding loudly as John's head disappeared, 'Tell them we will get to the Sittang before them. That should annoy them.' He chuckled and lay back on his bed smiling.

Rivalry between the two battalions was growing. Tall stories had been exchanged during the day, but beneath the friendly banter there was the serious intention to put up a good show.

A patrol, consisting of four men failed to return that evening. They were due back from the western sector before dusk, and their non-arrival caused anxiety and much speculation.

'I can't think why at least one man could not have got back. I don't like it at all,' John said gravely.

'It's very worrying, but there is no need to give up hope yet.

There are thousands of Japs in the area. It's quite possible that both patrols have been cut off until the Japs move,' Peter Reed said.

It was odd, Vic thought to himself, how we all value the lives of our men. A month or so ago, the loss of life was tragic and serious, but now even a patrol reported overdue, an event which was almost commonplace, is disastrous. We're soft, he thought and felt depressed. Softness is failure. But we're not failures. Why shouldn't they live? And us too? He smiled to himself. Hells bloody bells, what am I worrying about? They're having an Election at home!

'Where the devil is that patrol?' he demanded angrily, as his mixed up thoughts broke through involuntarily. He thumped the table as he spoke. John and Peter looked at him in astonishment.

'Take it easy, Vic,' John said soothingly.

The discussion was interrupted by the sound of firing from close range and bullets which came whining into the camp. About six or seven hit the thick tree outside the command post, and several ricocheted alarmingly off the steel footbridge over the railway line. In the darkness sleeping men stirred, and, muttering to themselves, grabbed their rifles and tommy guns and moved silently and calmly to take up their positions on the perimeter.

The Japs were in the jungle across the road. Several booby traps detonated in quick succession. Two machine-gunners on the perimeter firing on fixed lines, swept the jungle systematically from north to south; their rattle and the swish of the bullets hitting the undergrowth was comforting. Their first task done, the machine-gunners stopped and waited. There was an eerie silence, and no one moved or spoke until two muffled explosions from the enemy position broke the tension and provoked the machine-gunners into action again. Long bursts of fire continued for five minutes, and when the gunners paused, there was another very long silence.

'Order the Stand Down, we will have a look in the morning. It was probably a few Japs who had lost their way,' John ordered presently.

An hour later, a party of enemy estimated to be between one hundred and one hundred and fifty strong, were seen by a patrol to enter Seiktangin. Immediately, the mortars went into action, and the bombs exploded amid the startled Japs, who, surprisingly, stayed put. No further reports came in until just before first light. Then the radios became jammed with messages and the telephone buzzed continuously.

Vic and John collated the information whilst Peter and his Havildar marked up the situation map. Japs had crossed the road in two main columns, one to the north and the other in the area of milestone 127, and with those on the west, now formed a ring around Nyaungbintha. There were something like five hundred on the east and probably many more on the west of the road.

John, Vic and Peter, half dressed and unshaven, stood close together in the tiny command post. John's fingers drummed on the table, Vic's forehead was deeply furrowed, while Peter gazed at his handiwork with evident satisfaction. He had been on duty all night, and looked haggard and drawn, but his picture on the map was unmistakably clear.

'I don't get it at all,' John said. 'Why haven't they moved more to the east? They started crossing at nine last night, and some have only got as far as Thitpat; many are nearer. Then there are a lot quite close on the other side of the road who shouldn't be there, except for one reason.'

'An attack?' Vic spoke tersely. John nodded.

'But if they intended to attack, why didn't they do so under cover of darkness, or even at first light?'

'Get to the blower and give the alert,' John ordered, 'I'm going to see A Company.'

Five minutes later, a light machine gun opened fire and a solitary Jap fell dead across the barbed wire. A booby trap boomed twenty five yards from the road in the jungle, then there was dead silence and everybody waited with bated breath, tense and anxious, for the enemy to emerge from the jungle. But they didn't come.

It was decided to destroy all the enemy on the east of the road first. Then, if time permitted, those on the other side would receive attention, for these had several miles to travel before getting out of range. Those on the east had only to move a further four or five miles to escape and, since they were now static, so close to Nyaungbintha, their intentions were thought to be aggressive. The tactics were simple, and based on the slogan of 'find 'em, hold 'em, and hit 'em.' These few words formed the only English known to the majority of Indian other ranks, who well knew their meaning.

Outnumbered now by more than four to one, the battalion sailed into action in all directions. A watch of six listening patrols, each of two or three men, formed a half circle on the west about eight hundred yards from base, while the artillery aimed their guns to the south and east. Time was the essence of success. There were only about twelve hours available in which to dispose of all the enemy on the east before they attacked, or moved on toward the Sittang, and out of danger.

The company hurrying to the south brought down mortar fire on a party of Japs one hundred and thirty strong, caught them in enfilade with machine guns as they ran to escape the bombs and, without waiting to mop up, or search the dead, resumed their task of heading off the Japs in the villages of Seiktangin, Kywengon and Thitpat. All the enemy-occupied villages were under observation by a platoon, or by a patrol of three or four Sepoys, and at 0705 hours a systematic shelling of the Japs commenced.

Despite the open country, the observers had been able to take up their positions unseen by the enemy. Fortunately, it was raining cats and dogs, which provided excellent, if somewhat unreliable, cover and fairly wide detours by the patrols around to the rear of the Jap positions caught the enemy looking the wrong way. Those not actually manning their defences moved quite freely about the village, unconcerned, and unaware of danger.

Such scornful disregard for the efficiency of the 6th Punjabis was a little unwise, for it enabled the patrols to approach within three or four hundred yards and to bring down the shells when the targets were most favourable. There was a lot of enemy movement in the tiny village of Thitpat when a crump of over a hundred shells whipped through the air to burst like claps of thunder. Before the debris settled, the guns switched to fire at the unsuspecting enemy in Seiktangin. By this time, the surviving enemy in Thitpat had recovered to some extent from the first blow. It was decided to proceed with their annihilation without further delay.

When the shells exploded, two dozen Japs fled straight into the fire of the medium machine guns, and after an hour the rest dispersed in great haste toward Seiktangin, where, having been allowed to concentrate, they were again heavily shelled. Then they scattered to the south-west, running in ones and twos, until their staggering little figures became dots, swallowed up in the rain. It was a beautiful and heartwarming sight. Revenge was indeed sweet.

The enemy in Akyat received the same treatment, but on a heavier scale, for Mike Cooper brought the medium heavy artillery into use, and sixteen guns hammered the Japs with devastating effect. To escape the shells, they ran into the cross-fire of machine guns and rifles and fell by the score. When all was quiet, and when it was felt that the Japanese had been smashed, the patrols walked in to mop up and count the dead.

When darkness closed in with tropical suddenness only a few Japs remained alive, several had escaped into the open fields, but well over one hundred and fifty dead lay in and around the village. Of these, a fair number had killed themselves.

Whilst the two villages were receiving attention, a number of incidents happened elsewhere. A small patrol killed four Japs in the area just west of milestone 126. At Gonde, three prisoners were captured by the same patrol, who then resumed their tour, collected seven Jifs (Japanese inspired fifth columnists) and another prisoner or war before reporting back to base.

The Burmese brought in two more, and were rewarded at the stipulated rate of £1 per head. Locals also came with the news that one hundred and ninety odd Japs were killed in the shelling on Zaha and Leikpaw on the day before, but apart from these, who could not be claimed without corroboration, the day had yielded in total two hundred and twenty one enemy killed, ten prisoners of war and the seven Jifs. The battalion had suffered no casualties. The battle had developed into a massacre, but there were many more Japs to come. No one could relax.

Tired men went out to take up positions for the night. One company moved to Seiktangin, two platoons hid in Kywengon, and a dozen listening patrols laid up on the enemy's anticipated routes. In the wet and miserable night they took up their positions and settled down to wait. Within the hour the enemy were on the move, and following in the tracks of those who had previously crossed the road.

Such stupidity deserved the disaster which befell them. As they neared Seiktangin, the ambush company called for mortar and artillery fire. Except for several periods when the monsoon rain obscured the target, the bombardment continued throughout the night. Vivid gun flashes, blinding to the unshielded eye, lit up the night sky like lightning as the sweating gunners toiled hour after hour with clockwork precision. There was no rest for friend or foe.

When the rainstorms burst over the target area, the ambush men peered hard into the darkness to locate the Japs. The keen-eyed fired tracer bullets in mystic crescents, pinpointing the targets. Machine gunners crouched, adjusted gun barrels and let loose a stream of bullets over the paddy fields. Death came to the Japanese with the same sureness as that by which night follows day. The ambush commander called for shells and the guns never failed.

When the dawn came, the ambush company advanced cautiously. Seven Japs surrendered meekly, and glad, it appeared, to escape from the horror of it all. Seventy-three enemy corpses littered the immediate area and to the south-west dead bodies lay huddled in the mud and water. There were no wounded. Some enemy had escaped, but only to the villages beyond, where they were soon found and shelled again.

All day long, patrols trudged across the countryside from cover to cover and from village to village. Running fights developed in a dozen places.

Hundreds of dead were never found, but about one hundred and twenty enemy bodies were counted, and there was not sufficient time to search Thazi or Ohshitkon, both of which had been heavily shelled and undoubtedly contained a number of enemy killed. That night, there were fewer troops in ambush roles than on the previous nights.

The battalion had been in action continuously for the past forty-eight hours, and the men were mentally and physically exhausted. They had trudged through the quagmires of mud and water for mile after mile, had hurried into positions, crawling the last few yards and had stayed there tense, for long periods with all their faculties in deep concentration. At night, they had waited, staring into the nothingness of the night for hour after hour. Often, bushes and trees had moved suddenly and quickly and the area had become alive. Then, in the blink of an eyelid, everything was still again and the watchers, wet and amxious, stopped trembling and shrugged their shoulders. Only when they were actually firing were the soldiers able to relax from the tension.

No one had been able to sleep for two nights in succession, and gradually through June and July the tension had mounted to breaking point. Then it snapped and the men rejoiced, but in its place a new tautness came. Human beings cannot in any circumstances go out in the fields for the sole purpose of killing other humans without feeling the effects, and when the fields are flooded day after day, and night after night, and there is no sleep or rest and only the rain and darkness for comfort, the strain becomes overpowering.

John's decision to rest as many men as possible, for just one night, was wise. It allowed the men to recharge, in part at least, in preparation for the resumption of the battle which was only half won.

The officers at Nyaungbintha had just finished a scrappy evening meal and were about to relax for an hour when a series of small explosions shook the wooden shutters of their hut.

'There she blows,' the doctor joked.

'It's our booby traps going off,' Vic said. 'The noise wasn't far away. I reckon it was the rest of the grenades on the railway line, west of Kawamyaung.'

'I'm going to speak to Brian. He has only got one section in Kawamyaung. Warn Mike we will need some artillery soon,' John said, as he went over to the command post.

Before the guns opened fire, Brian had moved his H.Q. and a platoon from Leikpaw to Kawamyaung while the enemy column about two hundred strong, had moved from the railway to within four hundred yards of Brian's position. The moon provided sufficient light for Brian to see the dark patch of Japs struggling across the uneven flooded country. The first crump from the artillery was observed by him to be a bit off target, but with the correction, the next fell slap across the enemy column. Then the wireless failed, and in the hiatus which followed, D Company had some difficulty in keeping the Japs under control. The moon was fickle and disappeared for several minutes at a time behind dark clouds, which threatened to burst and put an end to the slaughter.

But the Japs became strangely immobile and lay on the ground where they were first shelled, apparently incapable of initiative and movement. To encourage them to remain static, D Company maintained spasmodic small arms fire in their direction and Vic laid on a repeat artillery bombardment.

In bright moonlight, the shelling continued. The enemy moved north, then south, and then east, but the guns, directed by Brian, found them every time. There was no escape until the rain came, and fell like a waterfall. The night became dark and the Japs were lost. Out in the quagmire west of Kawamyaung, the shattered remnants of the Japanese column struggled to their feet, muttered to each other in low tones, and slowly moved on toward the east.

Three hundred yards north of Kawamyaung, a listening post of three Pathans, Lance Naik Said Mohd and two sepoys, lay in a thicket. They had taken up their position at dusk and had seen the enemy approach. They had seen the shells burst in the mud and water, and had drawn closer together when the rain came. Soaked through to the skin, and alone in the open, the night for them was long. The hours of darkness after the noise of battle had ceased seemed endless, but the dawn was approaching and, in pouring, dense rain, it came hesitatingly at first as though afraid to see the slaughter of the night.

Said Mohd nudged his comrades. 'Look out there, there may be Japs about.'

They peered anxiously into the mist and watched the foreground gradually lengthen from five to twenty yards. Then they saw the enemy. Lots of them were lying on the ground twenty five yeards away. Recognition came to friend and foe almost simultaneously, but the Pathans were quicker. The tommy gun rattled, spitting bullets viciously, unerring in accuracy, and the Japs clung closer to the wet earth. One fired back, the bullet hit Said Mohd in the arm just below the elbow, narrowly missing the bone.

'Keep their heads down, I'll settle this,' he muttered and stood up, rifle on guard, bayonet fixed. He walked a few paces towards the enemy, broke into a trot, and as the nearest Jap fumbled feverishly with his rifle, Said Mohd sprang. His bayonet slashed through the Jap, his heavy muddy boots stamped hard on the body. He sprang again and again, a dozen times, from Jap to Jap, lying in the mud mesmerised by the Pathan's satanic fury. An officer rose to fight, Said Mohd swerved to avoid the lunging sword and brought the butt of his rifle down on the officer's skull with a crack like that of a whip. He charged on, oblivious of the enemy fire from his rear, shot two Japs who attempted to resist, was nearly blown to bits by a hara-kiri grenade attempt and, with only seven live Japs left, called for help. The three men swept towards the cluster of enemy, the tommy gun spat twice, and two bayonets flashed. All the enemy lay dead. Said Mohd walked over and reported to his company commander. 'Twenty five enemy killed Sahib.'

Later, when Brian told John, he said, 'I heard some firing and saw some movement through the rain, but I wouldn't believe it until I went over. There they were, one officer, two warrant officers, and twenty two privates, all as dead as doornails.'

In addition to the twenty five bodies, seventy more were found where the first shells had exploded and when D Company assembled to return to base, half a dozen forlorn and dazed Japanese private soldiers wandered over from the open paddy fields and sat down. The Pathans eyed them in a cursory manner and then resumed gathering the enemy weapons. Four machine-guns, and six officers' swords, together with a number of rifles and pistols had been collected when Brian abandoned the search. It was not a satisfactory way to end an action, but time was precious and the Pathans were needed at base where there had been intense activity. The enemy had been seen moving towards Ohshitkin and A and C Companies were in contact and calling for artillery. On their way to the village they had killed two enemy and captured three prisoners including one officer. They had then thrown a ring of men around Ohshitkin and bombarded the Jap with every available gun. The enemy were in strength and outnumbered the companies, who in total had one hundred and fifty men by two to one. Stubborn resistance by the Jap was unexpected but was met by vigour and aggression by the Sikhs and Jats.

The village provided some good bamboo cover against the shelling, which, although heavy and accurate, failed to dislodge the enemy. Mike Boon attacked. There was tough hand-to-hand fighting, then a bayonet charge drove the Japs into the east corner of the village. Here they held out and fought back in traditional style. Well led and organised, they were determined to survive. There was no sign of weakness, and no prisoners were taken. When darkness fell, the defiant Japs were still there in the corner of Ohshitkin and when the Sikhs and Jats were ordered to withdraw, a watchdog platoon of thirty men were left to keep contact with them. Over forty enemy had been killed and many more dead and wounded were without doubt lying in the Jap-held parts of the village.

While the main battle raged at Ohshitkin, a dozen smaller actions took place elsewhere. At milestone 131, a score of Japs sat astride the road at midday and took on all comers until the troops of tanks literally blasted them to bits. A patrol at the ford successfully ambushed a party of ten enemy and killed the lot. A dozen Japs appeared around the Nyaungbintha perimeter and defied all attempts to be shot or captured intil a bayonet party consisting mainly of cooks and clerks, dispersed them, killing six.

The artillery battery within the camp engaged targets to the west, north and east. The battalion's own mortars fired continuously, mainly into the jungle to the west, where the enemy were moving in force. No one knew what was really happening at any one particular moment for there was no time for lengthy appreciations or reconnaissances and the command post was an absolute madhouse. The wireless gurgled and crackled incessantly. When it rained, the railway bridge was used to obtain a better reception.

Between the frequent storms the sun came out and the atmosphere became hot and humid. Officers and men in and around the command post stripped to the waist and went about their jobs like men possessed. When the Japs appeared around the perimeter with aggressive intent and fired into the positions, no one stopped or ran for shelter. The sentries fired back from the safety of their gun positions and for a time they played a cat and mouse game with the enemy. Then it got out of hand and the noise inconvenient. John had found a V.C.O.

'Doing anything, Sahib?' he enquired gently.

'Not for the moment, Sahib, I'm going out on patrol in twenty minutes.'

'All right then, get hold of a party of odds and sods and go around behind those Japs and bump 'em off.'

'Right, Sahib.'

The deed was done, and relative quiet reigned again. As the information was collected and each party of Japs pinpointed, action was decisive and rapid.

At one time there were less than two dozen defenders to repel an attack on the base. The situation demanded immediate action in a dozen different places. Nothing else mattered. The

Japs could only be killed once and the battalion, now in the ascendant, forgot their weariness, their leaden legs and tired eyes. Every man fought with a reckless ferocity and beneath the fury, the enemy could only die.

During the afternoon, the missing patrol turned up and John was so relieved, he almost hugged them.

'Where have you been?' he enquired.

'Sahib, the adjutant sahib told us not to lose sight of any enemy we might find, and we have been following a party of two hundred since yesterday afternoon.

John could have added that at least one member of the patrol should have reported back to H.Q. in accordance with orders.

'Well done, you did very well,' he said.

B Company had a running fight with an enemy force thirty strong and killed twenty two before resuming their advance. When darkness came down, one hundred dead Japanese had been actually seen, another two hundred had been killed or wounded and there were nineteen prisoners. The battalion had sustained four wounded casualties. The day had been profitable.

At eight o'clock in the evening, when the night was quiet and the rain had ceased for the time being, Mike Cooper, the artillery major, brought an ammunition return for signature. After Vic had signed it, Mike said, 'Did you read the number you signed for?'

'Good Lord no, why should I? It's ridiculous anyway. What the hell does your H.Q. think we do with the shells if we don't use them? Sell them? We are only interested in killing the Jap and having enough ammo to do it with. What has been expended is of no consequence except to ascertain the amount to be replaced.'

'We must conserve artillery ammo. We have received instructions,' Mike replied in mock reproach.

'I'm more interested in conserving lives, and to hell with saving shells! Look what has happened today. We have bumped off well over three hundred of the little baskets without loss to ourselves,' Vic paused, 'that's the way to win wars. Let's have no stuff and nonsense about saving shells.'

'I don't know what the devil things are coming to. At home, they can afford the luxury of a general election, here we are asked to conserve shells,' Vic added good humouredly. 'Let's have a drink, we've earned it.' Then as an afterthought, 'By the way, how many shells have we used during the past twenty four hours?'

'More than you think. I'll tell you some other time. I want to enjoy this drink. What have you got?' Mike enquired as they entered the mess.

'Only the best I assure you. The very best Scotch, a good brandy, English gin, or if you prefer, some Nelson's Blood.'

A few moments silence was broken by Vic.

'Mike, did I see a railway engine come into the camp a few days ago, or was it my imagination?'

'Yes, you saw it all right. It came to take our billets away. You know all my blokes are living in the railway wagons on the siding? Well, ten days ago, a little man in railway uniform came in and wrote down all the wagon numbers and then, three days ago, in puffs the engine to take them away. Fortunately, by a freak of good fortune, all the rails between us and the main line were dislodged by the rain, and the engine returned without the wagons,' Mike said, adding, 'I am afraid there will be some trouble for you. You are in charge here, we're only the gunners.'

'I don't suppose by any chance, or perhaps by some mistake, that the men of the battery moved the railway lines? The rain story is a bit thin you know Mike!'

'Thin or not, that's your worry! This railway chappie came one afternoon with a notebook and by dawn next morning every blinking railway line on the siding had disappeared, except those the wagons were actually standing on. If they hadn't, I don't know what would have happened to us. There are no spare buildings. As it is, we are reasonably comfortable, and therefore able to give you first class support,' Mike said with a grin.

'Well, in that case, let's drink to the Burma Railways, and worry about the bill when it comes.'

No more shells were asked for that night, and the gunners slept soundly in their waterproof railway wagons. They had been in continuous action for sixteen hours.

Out in the darkness, patrols kept watch on the approaches and on the escape routes. The Punjabis waited silently in their ambush position at Kawamyaung. The rain fell fast and hard until well past midnight. Away in the depths of the jungle, columns of Japanese soldiers struggled eastward through the wet foliage, moving slowly and with difficulty towards the road. They were the remains of the Imperial Nipponese 28th Army. Their fortunes had fluctuated somewhat since they had swept through Burma proclaiming their invicibility, and since their ill-fated march on India. Now they sought only escape across the Sittang. Starving, festering with jungle sores and foot-rot, stricken with malaria and dysentry, they made their way painfully to the Nyaungbintha sector. Among them was their general, the G.O.C. 28th Army.

It was not until th early hours of the following morning that the Punjabis called for artillery fire. It was the same target area as the previous morning. In as many minutes, ninety eight Japs were killed and five surrendered. The rest, about one hundred strong, fled in disorder and as they ran, many dropped and died. Two elephants which had been lumbering along with the Japs stampeded, unfortunately in the wrong direction, and were last seen trumpeting their way to the Sittang.

The ambush had worked for the third night in succession in almost the same place, and when B Company returned to base at midday, they brought in twenty five rusty officers' swords.

'That's the nearest we will get to the headquarters of the 28th Army, twenty five swords and two elephants which got away,' Peter exclaimed.

'On the contrary,' John, his C.O. replied, 'there were a lot of officers in that party, which is indicative of an H.Q. There is plenty of time yet and somewhere out beyond our usual killing area the Japs are probably assembling again and moving east. We will have to find that place as soon as they have all crossed the road and we can afford to go after them.'

'It would be a feather in our cap if we could get the general,' Peter said.

'Yes, indeed! I'm going to have some food.'

But there was no lunch for the C.O. for an enemy force a hundred strong were reported moving east along the line of the Zaha Chaung, south of Nyaungbintha. A breathless Sikh burst in with the news. He and three others had trailed the Japanese for two miles, killing a dozen or so and when the column had been halted by the patrol fire, the sepoy had run to H.Q. leaving his comrades to shadow the enemy.

John decided that the Japs would not cross the road until after dark, and on this assumption, sent A Company to take up ambush positions in Inbintha for the night. Three Japs, presumably a patrol from the main column, were found lurking in the jungle a few yards from the perimeter wire and near a latrine. A sepoy coming out had stepped from behind the hessian screen and came face to face with the three Japs. They and the sepoy ran in opposite directions, the Japs stopped fifty yards down the track and were shot in the back by a small patrol which moved around to their rear, and found them looking the wrong way.

Peter Reed made an entry in the Game Book '1430 hours. Three enemy killed Nyaungbintha,' and continued receiving patrol reports.

Presently he spoke. 'I hate to mention it Vic, but we are running short of Japs.'

'How come?'

'Apart from the column moving towards milestone 127, there isn't a Jap within five miles on the west of the road and those Japs might well cross the road outside our area.'

'Hm, that is serious, but it had to happen some time. I'll see the C.O. How many Japs do we need for the target?'

'Counted bodies now amount to eight hundred and ten. That leaves us one hundred and ninety to get.'

'O.K.' Vic said as he went out to find his C.O.

John looked at the map for a few minutes before he spoke. 'What do you suggest Vic?'

'We have probably got our thousand, but only eight hundred and ten including prisoners have been actually counted. I suggest we go out to look for one hundred and ninety more so that there will be no possible doubt. Why not establish a forward base at Inbintha? A Company are already there. We could arrange supplies by air and patrol in force to the Sittang.'

'Good, that is what I had in mind, but what state are the men in? Do you not think I'm driving them too hard?'

'Not really. They are very tired. Who isn't? But I'm sure that the idea of going out after the Jap on a major scale will appeal to them.'

'O.K. then, I will go and see the Brig. at once and get his approval. He will have to get another battalion to relieve us here for a few days.'

The C.O. was back inside half an hour.

'The Brig. is tickled pink. He has arranged for a British battalion from 19 Div. to arrive here tomorrow morning, but we are to leave one company here,' he said enthusiastically.

'Will you please ask all officers to come to the mess immediately?'

15

TRIUMPH

Behind the column of soldiers, two bullock carts lumbered over the rough ground.

Now and then they stopped because a wheel got stuck behind a bund and they had difficulty in keeping close up to the soldiers. After about an hour, there was a long hold up when both wheels of one cart became solidly jammed behind a bund two feet high. Immediately there was an outburst of incoherent, vociferous shouts from the Burmese drovers as they prodded and prompted the bullock to pull harder, but it was to no avail for, as the fat beast heaved and grunted, the two wheels became more and more solidly stuck in to the soft mud. After a few minutes, the bullock half glanced behind, snorted loudly and derisively, and sank down gently into the water. His melancholy eyes blinked resignedly at the drovers. Consternation reigned among the Burmese. But not for long.

'Get that bloody animal on its feet,' an officer roared, 'get a dozen men under the wheels. Get a bloody move on. You're holding up the advance.'

The drovers shouted again, incoherent and loud. The men bent down, gripped, and heaved. The cart suddenly lurched forward and up on the bund where it stopped for a brief second before plunging down into the next field.

Mike Boon's report to the C.O. at Inbintha was not very hopeful. No Japs had been seen or heard since the previous evening and the Burmese, usually most helpful, had no information.

It looked very much as if the attempt to get a thousand enemy bodies was heading for a major flop. Too many battalions and units up and down the main road knew of the attempt for comfort. One, the senior battalion of the regiment were friendly but most anxious to score at the expense of the 6th. They would gloat and indeed they did, that very evening, when John spoke to them by wireless.

'We are sorry that you have had no Japs today. We have had a very good day, hundreds have been killed, some ran away in your direction, about six or seven. We do hope you will be able to find them.'

John was not daunted and gave orders for an attack on Yedwingon, a long smallish village a mile and a quarter to the north west, on the following day. Patrol reports received during the afternoon had not been promising; tracks and footmarks had been seen, but no Japs, so with more hope than certainty, the Sikhs, followed by the Jats and Tactical headquarters, disappeared into the rain on 27 July, leaving a rear party at Inbintha to receive the air drop which had been previously arranged.

Water two feet deep in many places prevented normal movement and the country was open, with only a few leafless bushes dotting the countryside. Caution was imperative. The speed of the advance was rather less than a thousand yards an hour. Presently, Mike Boon called a halt and tried to have a good look at the village which, standing on ground a little higher than its surrounding fields, appeared through the rain now and again as a dark mysterious huddle of trees, houses and sheds. No human movement could be seen and patrols went out to investigate. To the north, east and west of Yedwingon, little groups of Sikhs moved slowly and with great care and, when they returned, their reports were good. The village was full of Japs.

A Company moved forward again very slowly and gained the dry ground on the west of their objective. They crawled slowly up the gentle slope and within fifty yards of the edge of the village. There was a pause in the advance as machine-gunners crept into position on the flanks, and final whispered orders were passed from man to man. The rain had ceased and the only noise came from the gentle breeze as it stirred its way through the bushes and trees.

In the village, about two hundred enemy soldiers were resting. The Sikhs, fifty strong, and fifty yards away, started to move forward again. Almost imperceptively, hugging the wet ground, they crawled ten, twenty, twenty five yards, then up and in with a rush. An outburst of shouts, war cries, machine gun fire shattered the silence and quick as lightning, the first wave of Sikhs were in the village and a dozen Japs lay stone dead, with expressions of surprise on their faces. The first blood had been drawn, and the hunt was on.

Three sections went in with a dash, each gaining ground and each killing its path. Machine guns chattered incessantly, the noise now was deafening. The Japs fought back like cornered rats, but their grenades thrown in desperation and bullets fired in haste only spurred the Sikhs on to greater effort. These bearded warriors, now in their element, and with victory in their grasp, moved forward without fear, pity or remorse.

Through the village they stormed, from house to house and from tree to tree, shooting and stabbing with sure and deadly accuracy. Most of the Japs, caught unawares and unnerved, had only time to throw a quick grenade or fire a hurried shot before being killed. Some merely held the grenades to their stomachs, pulled the pin and thereby made the Sikhs' task easier.

There was a small group, a dozen strong, in position on the south edge of the village, who, from the cover of thick trees, flung a steady stream of grenades at their attackers. Here the advance was held up, but only for as long as the grenades lasted and when they had almost ceased, the section of Sikhs rushed the position. Only one Jap was alive, a very young woman. Around her, three other girls lay dead and she was about to throw her last grenade when a young Sikh grabbed her arm and retrieved the grenade. She broke into a torrent of incoherent abuse. The Sikhs grinned and took her to Company H.Q.

The attack had ended and the Jats of C Company came through to deal with the dozen or so Japs who remained alive, concealed in the village among the Sikhs. These were soon winkled out and offered only token resistance. Two, trembling and almost on the verge of tears, gave themselves up. The prisoners looked about, dazed and unable to believe their eyes. They had travelled a long way from the Arakan, had crossed the dangerous road and were within six miles of the Sittang and safety. Then, while they rested in the village of Yedwingon, Sikh soldiers had appeared from out of the open fields and charged with bullet and bayonet. In less than forty minutes the whole Japanese force had been destroyed. Only the prisoners, two men and one young woman, remained alive.

The female P.O.W. was interrogated first through the Burmese interpreter, and she was sitting in the corner of a hut when John and Vic went to see her. She wore a grubby ragged drill uniform and her face was dirty.

'I am not Japanese,' she cried, 'I am Chinese. I am the daughter of a bank manager who was in Rangoon before it was captured. See, here is my pass book.'

Three hundred thousand rupees stood to her credit. She was rich, she protested, and forced to go with the Japanese when they left Rangoon. She was pleased that the brave British had rescued her.

It was a credible story and indicated her quick recovery from her experience of the afternoon, but it did not matter. She was wholly Japanese. Her bank balance was undoubtedly impressive, the source of her fortune was unknown, though one could guess, but it was in Japanese currency and quite valueless.

'Take her to Inbintha and keep her under guard,' John ordered.

The battalion settled down for the night in the west edge of the village which had been cleared of enemy dead and which provided reasonable cover. Vic sheltered from the rain in a little lean-to hut. It smelt of pigs, chicken and Japs, but it was waterproof, and he slept like a log. Half an hour before daybreak, the men stirred and in ones and twos crawled and shuffled from their shelters into the grey damp dawn to make tea, strong and dark, under the dripping trees. The rain had ceased and the smoke from several little fires soon mingled with the humid air, and Vic wondered at the way the men ignited wet sticks and made them blaze.

He spoke by radio to Brian Rogers, still at Nyaungbintha, 'Good morning to you. I hope you've had a good night!'

'Like hell we have! Didn't get a wink of sleep. Bloody Japs were milling around all night,' Brian grumbled, adding, 'we killed twenty five.'

'Good show, that makes . . . ' Vic paused to tot up the score. 'We only need eight for our thousand.'

When he had finished talking to Brian, John said, 'Only eight to get, come let's walk through to the edge of the village. I'm sick of seeing dead and rotting Japs.'

'So am I. The stink of this place is awful and if the sun shines today, it will be unbearable,' replied Vic.

'I doubt whether we will get back here today. It depends on what we meet. We only need eight Japs. We may be lucky to meet a party nearby, but I think it is unlikely and we'll have to go on to Thongwale.'

They stood under the trees and looked towards Thongwale, a dark smudge against the background of the even fainter purple of the Siam hills.

'It's not far from the Sittang,' Vic said, 'and looks fairly big. Should have good cover for the night.'

They looked again at the vast flat expanse of water which stretched from their feet almost to the horizon, cold and uninviting. Here and there patches of scrub broke the surface and around them the water swirled, eddied and foamed, but these apart, the water was calm and still, secure in the network of bunds which formed a neat criss-cross pattern, monotonous and unending.

'Come, let's be off,' John said.

The men slipped and slithered on and off the muddy bunds and trudged and splashed through water two feet deep. The light was grey and the air still, as in single files they moved slowly toward the east and to the village which arose from the flood, seemingly as far away as ever.

Presently, a breeze sprang up, breaking the calm of the still water into row after row of tiny ripples which rolled across the surface to disappear into the northern bunds. There was a shout from the rear, 'Rain, Rain.' The men stopped, turned, and saw the storm swallow the flooded countryside as it swept in from the south, driven by great gusts of wind.

'Close up and advance!' John rapped, as the rain closed in upon them. The morning became very dark and Vic felt a moment of panic. 'Watch for an ambush in the scrub, we can't see beyond a few yards. We are a sitting target,' he shouted.

The men, with heads down, forced their way through the driving rain, into deeper water thick with weeds which clung to the ankles and legs, hindering movement. There was a complete stop as they came to a river, its banks almost disguised by the flood water, but after a moment's hesitation, the men, with weapons held aloft, waded slowly through the chest high water, and scrambled up the slippery bank on the far side.

John breathed relief as he and Vic stood on the bank, shaking out the surplus water.

'The current was worse than I thought. Some of the shorter men had trouble keeping on their feet,' Vic said.

The rain ceased, the water became shallower and the pace correspondingly quicker. Suddenly, a shot rang out and everyone stopped, suddenly, as if frozen. There was a moment of silent uncertainty as every pair of eyes searched the leafless yet dense prickly scrub. Nothing could be seen except bushes, bare, dark and half submerged by the water which swirled around them and on to the river, leaving a muddy brown froth clinging to the lower branches.

With an ear-shattering clatter, a Bren gunner, firing from the hip, sprayed the bushes from left to right. Two tommy gunners moved forward, and immediately spotted a Jap. He was perched precariously in a bush which bowed under his weight almost to the point of breaking. His feet dangled in the water. He was dead. His body was riddled with bullets. 'See this, Sahib!' The havildar passed over the Japanese rifle to John and Vic. One round had been fired, the rifle bolt was in the forward position and the combined efforts of the three men failed to pull it back. It was rusted solid.

'He must have put that round up the spout months ago and not touched it since,' Vic said.

'Their discipline has very obviously reached a low level but what did he hope to achieve? Why didn't he surrender instead of firing one abortive round? And who ordered him to stay here?' John queried.

It seemed odd, indeed, that the Jap should remain alone, without food, concealed in a bush in the middle of a vast flood, when, since no other British troops had previously been within miles of the position, he could easily have scuttled off eastwards to safety.

'Judging by his expression, and his physical condition, I doubt whether he knew what he was doing, and his instinct provoked him to fire,' was one suggestion.

'Let's get on,' John said impatiently. 'We need another seven Japs.'

When they arrived within striking distance of the village at about 1400 hours and John sent A Company to take up a position on its northern end with one platoon around to the east, the remainder prepared to sweep the area from south and north.

Seven Japs were surprised sitting in a house. One, an officer of field rank, who was six feet tall and broad, received the somewhat doubtful distinction of being probably the last officer to be killed in combat. The rest, thirty six in all, were killed in as many minutes.

Vic watched the attack go in. Usually, when an attack was on, he moved with it or sat in tactical headquarters with earphones on. Generally, every moment was tense and anxious, but today, only the first few moments were. The rest were calm and composed. For the most part, the attack was steady and unhurried, calm and remorseless. There was the steady chatter of Bren guns. Vic could smell the cordite from the gun a few yards to his left. He noticed the smooth, automatic charge of gun magazines and the pleasant almost benign expressions on the wet faces of the gunners. The rifle fire was all one way. The Japs who moved to defend were too late and those who had ample warning seemed to be mesmerized and fumbled too long. Six or seven killed themselves.

In forty minutes the task was complete, and the soldiers were moving back, still in open formation, unharmed and unhurried. The massacre of the breakout was over.

John and Vic went to the edge of the village. About a mile away, the water ended, and the purple foothills rose dark and forbidding from the far bank of the Sittang river which was indistinguishable in the distance from the floods.

'I wonder how many Japs are in those hills?' John mused, searching the area through binoculars.

'I wouldn't know, but what matter? They are half dead and won't be fit to fight for months.'

'It must be a hell of a blow to their morale. They have been well and truly defeated in battle, cut off in the hills for months without food and medical supplies, and then bombed, shelled, shot at time and time again, and harassed to hell.' John waved a hand in the direction of the bodies. They hadn't got any heart left to fight and neither would any other human being,' he added.

'Yes, I can feel almost sorry for the baskets. To be caught after getting here within sight of escape, it must have been heart breaking, but they could have surrendered months ago,' Vic rejoined.

'The little so-and-so's never surrender, our prisoners are only the lame and weary and the half dead, anyway. What next?'

A moment of silence, then Vic suggested, 'Our job is done. We are wet and tired. I think we are quite justified in going back.'

Vic should have felt elated. The battalion, at fifty percent below strength, had in ten days killed and captured over a thousand Japs, with the loss of only two sepoys. His friend's first command had been highly successful and it was extremely doubtful whether similar results had ever been obtained in any theatre of war. As they walked back to the assembled men, however, Vic's thoughts were sombre, his heart unaccountably heavy. He felt, at the very moment when pride and joy was appropriate, depressed and desolate.

A spell crept over him, making him aware of the gross stupidity of war, of man fighting man like beasts of the field. It was, perhaps, a culmination of events and incidents during the past few days. The handful of prisoners whose flesh on their feet came off with their socks; the Japanese women who fought like men; the Jap crouched in a bush, dying from hunger and fatigue, and whose only weapon was a rusty rifle; or dozens of other miserable experiences, all against the background of rain, mud, water and floods.

After a short rest, the battalion started off on their way back to Inbintha to spend the night.

There was no point in taking precautions for the area was quite clear of Japs, so they moved in close formation. Almost at once the rain started, and swept straight into the faces of the men who, with stout hearts, forced their tired bodies through the water and over the muddy bunds against the gale. The five miles were covered in five hours and it was dark when they reached Inbintha.

A warm and friendly welcome awaited. The industrious Burmese had helped the quartermaster to prepare hundreds of gallons of hot water and had used their own precious fuel to dry the clothing left in the village two days previously.

A room was put at Vic's disposal and on the stone floor stood a large basin of warm water, with soap and towels. Slowly, he pulled off his wet clothing, and examined his body. When the battalion had halted to cross the river, he had seen the shoals of wriggling leeches in the water. A few moments later he had shuddered involuntarily as several bit into the calves of his legs. Now, seven hours later, he inspected the damage.

The leeches, swollen with blood, fat and slimy, were still there, three on each leg in the neat formation of an arrowhead. He lit a cigarette from the candle and gently touched each leech with the burning tip until they squirmed, let go, and fell on to the floor. As he sat in the basin he smiled at the recollection of an Army Instruction which suggested that troops in leech infested areas should carry a little bag of salt with which to remove leeches from the body. Dry salt, of course! He dabbed the sore places in his legs with disinfectant, threw away the cigarette and poured the warm water over his body. Then he changed into his clean and dry uniform, and reported to his commanding officer.

'I have an idea there will be a reception committee awaiting us at Nyaungbintha. I think perhaps a little "bull" is indicated! he said.

'I think you are right about the reception, the brigade major wants to know our time of arrival,' John replied.

John entered the mess some ten minutes later beaming all over his pink face.

'The Brig. is pleased with us,' he announced. 'I have been asked to congratulate all ranks.'

John continued, 'In the morning, I intend to thank the men for the grand show they have put up and for their support of me on my first command. May I thank you, too, from the bottom of my heart.' John spoke quietly with obvious sincerity.

'Here's to the C.O.' someone said, and the toast was drunk.

John stood up again, his pink face slightly flushed.

'There will be a reception committee waiting for us at the camp. Don't know who will be in it, but we can assume that the two brigadiers, and perhaps the general, will be there. I think we ought to put up a show. Vic will give you the details.'

Vic stood up. 'I am sure you will agree that having achieved such a reputation for fighting we cannot just drift back into camp by sections,' he said.

'We have, therefore, arranged for the *dhol* and *surnais* (pipes and drums) band to meet us this side of Nyaungbintha, where the battalion will halt and form up in threes and tidy up. We shall then march in parade ground manner along the south edge of the village, until we meet the railway, when we will right turn and march along the railway into the camp. Warn the men to watch out for the order "Eyes Left!" I am assuming that the reception committee will be standing on the piece of open ground outside the booking office. A British battalion from 19th Div. is in Nyaungbintha, the Brigade H.Q. from 19th Div. and there are, of course, our very old friends, the gunners. I think we ought to show them all, and the V.I.P.s how the Punjabis of 17th Div. return from battle. It won't take much effort, but please put your men in the picture.'

Vic sat down amid murmurs of approval.

At about a quarter to twelve on the next day, the battalion were within four hundred yards of the appointed rendezvous with the band, whose six members could be seen waiting beneath the trees which bordered the village. Vic had hurried ahead by himslf to give them orders and was almost a furlong in front of the main party. He felt pleased and proud. The weather had been unusually kind as no rain had fallen during the morning and everybody had been able to keep their uniform and equipment fairly neat and clean. The plan for a grand entry into camp was nearing fruition. The battalion had completed an arduous two months monsoon fighting, had been out on a four day patrol, but notwithstanding, would march into Nyaungbintha looking like guardsmen on parade. He smiled in anticipation of the surprise that was in store for the reception committee, the gunners and the battalion who occupied the village. 'We will show them, what a war-time, mixed-religion battalion can do,' he thought.

He failed to see a deep ditch, whose banks were hidden by the floods. He stepped right into it, lost his balance, and staggered about half blind as the muddy water splashed his glasses. His bush hat drifted gently down stream right side up, and came to rest against a bush. As he struggled to regain his breath and balance, a wave of laughter came to his ears. He stood up, his body bent double, with legs apart, allowing the water to cascade from pockets, pouches and haversack. His uniform, covered with a black mud, clung to him like a wet dishcloth. He shuddered in disgust at the revolting sight. He shook his hat and, gingerly, placed it on his head. He groaned as a stream of water shot from his rifle and he heard the chuckles of laughter from the battalion who had now closed to about seventy yards.

His antics had been seen by most of the men and now Vic

realised that he, the adjutant whose job it was to ensure a good turnout, and who should set a shining example and had exhorted everybody to make a special effort on this auspicious occasion, was the only scruffy man on parade! Far worse, he was filthy, bedraggled, and smelling like a sewer. But he could not let the incident divert him from his purpose so, giving his clothes a final shake, he waved to the battalion, trying hard to be casual.

There was a few minutes break while all ranks tidied themselves and then the march into Nyaungbintha started.

The right wheel at the railway line was accomplished in good style and John, six paces in front, headed along the straight towards the reception committee who stood on the open ground wher expected.

Vic, a few yards behind John, cast an anxious eye over his shoulder and felt relieved as he saw the straight rows of men swinging along to the tune of a stirring march played by the pipes and drums. It was going to be all right, the march past was going to be a success.

John had about seventy yards to go, the battalion were all on the straight and passing the artillery, when, without warning, the guns opened fire, barely four yards from the column of troops whose immediate action was to dive for cover. Disorder threatened, the step was broken, and for a few seconds everybody bobbed along like an army of refugees. They recovered sufficiently to give an 'eyes left' to the brigadier although the rhythm had been lost and many men were still out of step. The salute by the gunners was unexpected and naturally startled everyone but, notwithtanding, the gesture was deeply appreciated.

It was a proud battalion which was dismissed a few minutes later. The brigadier congratulated all ranks on having achieved the target of one thousand Japs, and thanked them for their efforts.

Vic changed his clothes and wrote this summary of operations:

TO FLEW FORCE
SITUATION REPORT 109 TO 1600 HOURS 30 JULY STOP BATTALION RETURNED NYAUNGBINTHA 1240 HOURS STOP SUMMARY OF OPS 20–30 JULY STOP ENEMY BODIES COUNTED 981 STOP POW

INCLUDING ONE OFFICER ONE FEMALE 53 STOP TOTAL 1034 STOP ESTIMATED ENEMY CASUALTIES BELIEVED MANY MORE AS RESULTS MANY ARTILLERY SHOOTS NOT KNOWN STOP KNOWN ENEMY OFFICER CASUALITIES 40 INCLUDING ONE MAJOR STOP 42 SWORDS 14 MACHINE GUNS MANY SUBMACHINE GUNS RIFLES CAPTURED OR DESTROYED STOP OWN CASUALTIES 2 KILLED 15 WOUNDED STOP ARTILLERY PARTICULARLY 311 FIELD BATTERY SUPERB DURING WHOLE PERIOD STOP THEIR SUPPORT AND CLOSE COOPERATION RESPONSIBLE FOR LARGE NUMBER OF ENEMY KILLED STOP 9TH JATS M.M.G.S. 20 DIV WERE EXCELLENT AND MOST ENTHUSIASTIC STOP

16

THE END

On 2 August a score of P.O.W.s were brought into headquarters, most of whom had been handed over by the villagers. All were in a most distressed condition, thin, weak from hunger and exhaustion and suffering from terrible sores and foot-rot. They looked a sorry lot.

'Get 'em away quick to Div. H.Q. before they get too much pity,' John ordered Vic, and away they went, within twenty minutes after their arrival.

Men not actually on patrol or duty were ordered to rest, sleep periods were organised by companies, and after the struggles of the past few weeks, everybody looked forward and expected at least a week's rest.

It was not to be. During the afternoon of 2 August, a brief message was received warning the 6th Punjabis to relieve their own 4th battalion at Pyabyo near Waw, eighty miles to the south. The news was received with mixed feelings. Some of the older soldiers of the battalion who had spent some years in the 4th prior to 1941 welcomed the opportunity to meet old friends and comrades. Those, including the many officers who had no ties with the 4th, were not at all keen. Vic protested to the C.O.

'It's a bit thick John. There are less than half a dozen battalions in action now. We have had a pretty rough passage for two months and done much more fighting than any other unit. We are all tired and need a few days' rest before we start again. Surely there are other battalions available!'

'Yes, but orders are orders, and whilst I feel that we are overdue for a rest, we will have to go. I'm not too happy about it though,' was John's reply.

'Well, I think we ought to make some sort of protest. Would

you mind if I phoned division and make some enquiries? I can do it unofficially, and you needn't know.'

'Yes, all right, but be careful,' said John.

A pleasant voice answered Vic's call to the divisional G branch, and he assumed it was the G.I.

'I have received your message warning us to move to relieve our 4th battalion. I am wondering if it is a mistake?' Vic spoke smoothly.

The voice said, 'No, it was not a mistake.'

'But surely we are due for a few days' rest. We are very much under-strength, have a lot of foot-rot, and we would feel much happier if we could move in, say a week's time,' said Vic, adding hastily, 'don't musunderstand me, everybody is naturally quite pleased about meeting up with our 4th, but I don't think we are in a fit state to go into action again so soon.'

The voice was extremely pleasant, and said it appreciated only too well the amount of hard work done by the battalion, and in the very difficult conditions. Had the choice been his, it was doubtful whether the battalion would have been selected for the job, but a very special request from 7 Div. H.Q. had been received asking that your battalion should be sent. 'Apparently,' the voice went on, 'your 4th battalion made the original request, and we felt that we must meet their wishes. After all, not all battalions are in such demand and it's obviously a great honour.'

There was no answer to that, and Vic replied, 'Well, I took a very poor view of the proposed move at first, but since you put it like that, I'm sure we'll be delighted to go. I hope you don't mind me troubling you.'

'Not at all,' the voice said, still very pleasant. 'I appreciate your point of view, and wish you much more good hunting.'

Vic passed the news to John. 'Well, in that case we will be pleased to go. We have shown our mettle to the senior battalion, and we will now show the 4th how to deal with the Japs,' he said.

The 6th battalion was very junior, having only been formed in 1941, whereas both the lst and 4th were regular units and, of course, very much aware of their status, but the 6th had won an excellent reputation recently under the very eyes of their elders, and John, the acting officer commanding, was pleased about the opportunity to display his battalion to the 4th, which was his own original battalion.

Instead of starting a well deserved rest, the 6th spent 3 August overhauling weapons and equipment, and packing for the move. During the afternoon, Brigadier Flewit made a very thoughtful gesture by thanking all ranks for their support and effort while under his command, and wished them well in the future.

Next morning, when the battalion was ready to move off, he appeared and shook hands with all commissioned officers, who were deeply touched by his sincerity, and felt a little reluctant to leave his command which, although very short and barely a fortnight long, had been sufficient to achieve a remarkable degree of understanding. The truck engines were running, the troops were all aboard, so last goodbyes were said. The convoy moved off to a new area and new friends. Their old friends, the British gunners, stood by the roadside and waved them on their way. Many hearts were sad.

Pyabyo lay on the west side of the Sittang Old Channel. To the east of the village there was nothing but floods hiding numerous tributaries of the Sittang river, and a few isolated villages. It was on dry land, but only just, for the flood water lapped the defensive positions. On its south edge, there was a large wooden building built high on stilts, and almost on its northern boundary a stone tower stood about one hundred feet high. The only other notable feature of the village was the smell, particularly after rain. It was a foul stench of sewerage. A lot of soldiers, friend and foe, had stayed there.

The present inhabitants, the 4th Punjabis, were glad to see the 6th and extended a royal welcome. There was sincerity and friendliness, and Vic's conscience worried him a bit as he thought of his protest against the move. Old friends were united, old comrades met and talked; there were smiles and happy faces. There was line shooting on an unprecedented scale, but not for long for there was work to be done.

On the east side of the Sittang Old Channel and about three miles from Pyabyo, the enemy held a number of villages in strength and by all accounts were tough and aggressive. Intelligence had estimated that in the whole of the Mokpalin area the Jap forces numbered almost fifty thousand. The port of Moulmein was at their disposal.

The villages occupied by A and B Companies dominated no-man's land. The enemy had recently made several abortive attempts to capture them, and that night, a few hours after the arrival of B Company, they made a determined attack. In the darkness and in strange surroundings, the Punjabis stood fast, held their fire until the last moment and then put the enemy to flight with small arms fire. B Company's casualties were light and the Japs removed all traces of theirs before dawn.

This incident acted as a tonic, and immediately the care and maintenance attitude, which threatened efficiency, gave way to aggressive action.

'I'm not having this sort of thing happening in my area,' John announced abruptly at breakfast, and for the next week the patrolling was carried out at maximum strength. The whole area was swept and searched several times. At every opportunity, the enemy held villages were heavily shelled.

The incidence of foot-rot became steadily worse and the doctor grumbled incessantly, 'How can I keep the men fit when every other day every man is walking through two feet of water?' he protested.

A game of hide and seek soon developed in the three mile wide corridor of country which separated the two occupied areas. One day, battalion H.Q. woke up to find that the Japs had advanced, and occupied a small undefended village. Efforts to dislodge them were unsuccessful at first, so it became necessary to occupy another village behind them, whereupon the Japs, deterred by heavy and accurate shell fire, withdrew.

The enemy activity was worrying, their aggressive attitude caused concern. It seemed that the Jap movements were in preparation for an attack. The brigadier talked of mounting an attack on the Jap main positions, a prospect which appealed to no one else, for the country was flat, offered practically no cover, and was flooded to a depth of two to three feet. The enemy were well dug in, outnumbered the British forces by about six to one, and obviously intended to stay put. The brigadier, newly appointed, personally patrolled the whole front on foot, a feat which earned him great respect but gained no enthusiasm for his attack. John, who had accompanied him on the patrol, voiced his apprehension between dinner and poker on evening to his senior officers.

'He is certainly keen to attack, and talks of nothing else, but for the life of me, I really cannot see what hope there is of success. The country is wide open all around the Japs, and we would have to cross the old channel, which is three or four feet deep.'

Vic put in a word, a trace of anger in his voice. 'If he orders an attack, we will have to put up a good show, but I would feel much happier if we were up to strength, and fit. Our men are tired, and of our total strength, of five hundred, over fifteen percent are suffering from foot-rot. I don't believe the men are in the mood for an attack of this sort. Give 'em a rest for a fortnight away from these bloody floods, and it might be a proposition. They have been soaked to the skin practically every day for the past ten weeks.'

'An attack by night would have more chance of success, but it would be difficult to achieve surprise because of the noise we would make moving through the water,' said Brian, adding, 'Our main trouble is that the Japs here are much tougher and in a real fighting condition, not like those we met at Nyaungbintha.'

'Yes, I have noticed a tendency on the part of many of the men to be over optimistic, and as a result, a little careless. We must impress upon them that the enemy here is a different kettle of fish,' said John.

The days of August '45 passed very slowly. The monsoon continued, and the village smelt worse than ever after each storm. Patrols became more and more ambitious, and on several occasions, penetrated between the Jap forward positions and managed to get within a hundred yards of the main enemy position. A great deal of valuable information was gained reflecting great credit on the patrol members, whose task was extremely hazardous, but after a little experience they became quite adept in getting behind the enemy position, even though their route was through flood at least two feet deep which made the going both slow and dangerous!

It usually took the whole night for a patrol to cover three miles. There was not much cover, only a few isolated bushes and trees, and enemy patrols came out night after night and had to be avoided. It was not always dark enough, and when the moon came out suddenly, the patrols could only "freeze" where they stood in order to escape detection, their hearts thumping madly, while cold shivers and hot tinglings ran up and down spines, arms, and along the backs of their fingers.

The more imaginative saw in their mind's eye a grim-faced

Jap, perhaps only two hundreds yards away, slowly moving the sinister barrel of his machine gun with all the time in the world, taking careful aim, while a stubby damp finger tightened on the trigger, squeezing gently till the barrel spat an arc of bullets and death!

More often than not, the patrols were undetected, but on a few occasions, an alert Jap sentry saw the strange silhouettes, blinked, and then whispered in the darkness to his comrades. Often, fleeting clouds came to the rescue of the patrol, who moved on in relative safety. On several nights however, the machine guns opened fire, and the patrols went to ground and crawled furiously through the mud and water and out of range. There were no fatal casualties but a number of men were wounded. Every day the enemy positions were shelled, and frequently the artillery opened fire when it was felt that the Japs would present a good target. Special efforts were made to interrupt their meals.

Between 7 and 12 August, the villages of Posabe and Pannyo changed hands several times without any casualties on either side.

On the following day, the brigadier came to tea, and hinted that in some quarters there were rumours of a Japanese surrender. No one paid much attention. Much later, after he had gone, and the evening meal was in progress, the atom bomb was discussed, and several officers expressed their views on the controversy which appeared to be raging at home and in the U.S.A.

'I can't understand why people should object to its use, when it is obviously intended to end the war, but then I suppose there are thousands of people who have made a good thing out of it, and I suppose that they are the very ones who don't want to see it finished,' said Vic with a touch of bitterness.

'You are dead right,' Brian replied, adding, 'we could do with an atom bomb on the Sittang to finish off the Japs, who, I think will never surrender.'

'Yes, Brian, just a teeny weeny one, sufficient to blow all the Japs sky high!' Vic agreed.

'Surrender is a lovely thought, but I think Brian is right, they will never surrender,' said John quietly.

Rumours about the possibility of a Japanese surrender grew stronger during the next day or so, and they had a disturbing effect on both officers and men, who almost at once became unsettled and irritable. An order from S.E.A.C. H.Q. forbidding offensive action on the east of the Sittang was received and obeyed. The cheerful attitude which had held the battalion together as an efficient fighting unit for so long, diminished.

At 0815 hours on 15 August, the Japs withdrew from Pobyan, a village which they had occupied for some time, and it seemed at the time that the Japanese withdrawal indicated that their surrender was imminent. Hopes ran high, but for the next two days there was no sign of a capitulation, and in the heavy rain which only ceased for an hour or two during the forty eight hours, a feeling of despondency was borne in Pyabyo. It did not persist, for at first light on 18 August a fairly large party of Japs pushed a patrol out of Pobyan and into the open paddy fields.

'What we have, we hold,' John had said a dozen times, and now a group of houses and a tree had been lost. He gave his orders, concise and to the point.

'Pabyan will be retaken by nightfall.'

Reinforcements were despatched within minutes. An artillery fire plan was coordinated and shells were whistling overhead within twelve minutes and continued off and on for an hour, but the enemy refused to budge and the original patrol, together with the reinforcements advanced to the village under a creeping barrage of shells. The Japs then withdrew, in an orderly manner.

There was much speculation regarding the intention of the enemy, and while, according to the radio, the war was now over, there was no sign whatever of a local surrender.

The strain became almost unbearable. Men lay awake at night, wondering, trying to sort out conflicting facts, and trying so desperately to form a sensible conclusion. On the one hand, there was the atom bomb, and subsequent announcements that the war had ended. With that, came a vision of life, good food, a comfortable bed, civilisation, entertainment, dry clothes, and above all, leave and home.

Supposing the Japs remained stubborn and continued to fight, and it appeared certain that they would? What then? More months of slogging through mud and floods, soaking clothes, prickly heat and foot-rot, more mepacrin, more Japs to find and more to kill, more tinned food, peas and beans, tasteless and soggy, more sleepless nights on hard beds, damp and uneven, and the awful tiredness and aching of limbs, perhaps even the brigadier's suicidal attack across flat and flooded country.

A surrender offered life; no surrender offered existence, perhaps death. There was much in the balance and only the Jap could tip the scales. But could we not help him to tip them? Could we not use persuasion?

Such were the thoughts of the men in that water-logged village of Pyabyo during the first days after the war had officially ended.

A 'surrender reaction' attempt carried out in the adjacent sector had not been a success. Four dummy men, lifelike and with white flags were placed in a jeep, which, without tyres, was placed on the single track railway line which ran eastwards from the British to the Japanese position, down a slight incline.

Some leaflets to tell the enemy that the war was over were placed in the jeep, which was given a good shove by many willing hands. It started slowly, gathered speed, and literally careered down the railway line on the embankment toward the most forward Japanese positions. It arrived within about seventy yards undamaged, but a moment later it was evident that the Japs were not prepared to cooperate. Their comparatively small detachment at the culvert position threw everything at the jeep which, battered by grenades, and torn by bullets, its dummy men in shreds and swaying drunkenly, sailed on and disappeared into the dead ground.

The incident strengthened the opinion, now widely held, that a Japanese surrender was unlikely. Brigade H.Q. telephoned incessantly asking for information concerning enemy movement and in the rear Corp and Army H.Q. waited impatiently for a sign of surrender.

Johnny Loosemore, the war correspondent, and an old friend of the battalion, appeared without warning on 22 August, and was warmly welcomed. The situation at the Sittang Bend area had considerable news value, probably much more than any other area, and it was pleasing that Johnny Loosemore should be on the spot to obtain the potential scoop, and particularly so because no other correspondent had shown any interest in the area or in the battalion. He was made comfortable and later joined the officers in the mess for a meal.

By nine o'clock or thereabouts, the arguments ceased by common consent and the officers settled down to a quiet game of poker, which became carefree as the hours passed and as more liquor was consumed. The session was not by any means a drunken orgy but those who drank were not quite as cautious as usual and perhaps were seeking escape from the tension.

In the circumstances, there was perhaps nothing exciting or unusual in the scene; just a group of off-duty officers seeking to relax, and making the best of the conditions. They were all young and remarkably well turned out, in clean and starched uniforms and wore neat neckerchiefs which added a dashing touch to their green drill battledresses.

With the exception of the three Sikh officers, all were freshly shaven, and their general appearance was clean and smart. Each had swallowed something like five hundred yellow mepacrin tablets at the rate of two a day during the campaign and their complexions were sallow and almost like those of the Japanese, but they were fit and healthy, even though cheekbones were prominent and their faces drawn and thin.

Their surroundings were dingy but the atmosphere was warm and friendly. The dozen officers sat around the end of a very large table which stood in the corner of a room the size of a tennis court. The wooden walls were discoloured with age and neglect and in several places grey army blankets hung precariously, hiding the cracks and windows and preserving the blackout. Over the table, two car bulbs swayed gently and cast a flickering circle of illumination. A solitary bulb dangled over the command post fifteen paces away and, in its light, enclosed by a hessian screen, an orderly talked in low undertones with the telephone operator.

The rest of the huge room was in complete darkness, concealing bedding rolls and a quantity of Buddhist religious symbols. No windows were open and smoke from pipes and cigarettes rose steadily towards the raftered roof.

The play was comparatively quiet, bids were made in low voices and only an occasional outburst of laughter followed by a ribald remark broke the low murmur of conversation. The hours passed pleasantly until just after eleven o'clock, when Vic stood up.

'Leave me out for a while. I must get the patrol reports,' he said, and walked over to the command post.

Seating himself at the trestle table, Vic rang a forward patrol base and spoke to the N.C.O. in charge.

'Have you seen any Japanese?'

'There is some firing to the north, Sahib, and about half an hour ago we saw a party of Japs moving westwards.'

Vic raised his voice. 'How many Japs did you see?' He became aware of the hush which had fallen over the poker school. The N.C.O. replied, 'About a dozen or so.'

Vic picked up the situation map, studied it for a moment, and returned to the group of officers who looked up expectantly.

'It's all right, there is nothing to worry about,' Vic grinned, 'at least, not yet.'

He pointed out the position of the reported enemy movement.

'In normal circumstances,' he said to the C.O. 'one wouldn't bother but may I suggest, sir, that it is quite possible that the Japs heading towards us may be part of a much larger movement, which may be a threat to our position here, and since, in any event, the Jap movement is aggressive, we should take action.' A smile spread over his face.

'Aggressive! How do you mean, Vic?' John asked quietly.

'Well sir, the - ' Vic's explanation was interrupted by John.

'Of course, Vic, I see it quite clearly now. Supposing that Jap patrol is the advance force of an enemy attacking party. Good heavens, why we may even be attacked here! How many Japs were seen?' John looked up at Vic, and there was a twinkle in his eye.

'About a hundred,' Vic replied without batting an eyelid.

'That's better. But what do you suggest, Vic? I don't feel justified in sending out a company on a wild goose chase at this time of the night.'

'I suggest some gentle shelling, say seventy or eighty rounds here for an hour, then a repeat here, then the same here, and then we could start again.'

'But those places are all the Jap occupied villages east of the Sittang.'

'Yes, I know, but the shelling will break the boredom, and we are quite justified in using the guns because the enemy are being aggressive, and,' Vic paused and lowered his voice, 'we will know in the morning whether the Jap intends to surrender or not. The shelling will do them good.'

The C.O. looked up into Vic's quite expressionless face and smiled.

'I understand perfectly Vic,' he said.

It only took a few minutes to lay on an artillery fire plan to start in about ten minutes. The poker game started again, and glasses were refilled. As the artillery officer rejoined the group, Vic raised his glass.

'Sir, gentleman, let us drink to the health of our gunners. They always get us out of trouble.'

Play had been in progress again for about five minutes when the shells began to pass overhead, their whistles barely audible above the sound of the rain. There was a moment's pause as the officers listened, and then Vic broke the silence.

'Any moment now the telephone will ring and the angry voice of our brigade major will demand to know what the hell we are doing. You may all take comfort from the fact that we have the perfect answer. Whose deal is it?'

In fact, it was well over half an hour before Brigade H.Q. tumbled to the fact that one of their battalions was shelling the Jap, and, shelling hard. The brigade major demanded angrily, 'What the hell are you doing?'

'Why, shelling the Jap of course,' Vic replied quietly.

'But surely you are aware of the S.E.A.C. order that there must be no aggressive action on our part!'

'Certainly, but this is purely defensive fire. There is a lot of Jap movement on our front and, therefore, the fire is quite justified. What are we to do? Wait and be attacked?' Vic enquired gently.

'Well no, but you should have contacted brigade first,' the B.M. said.

'But we have the authority to use the divisional artillery,' Vic paused. 'If you are going to give us the order to stop firing, naturally we will do so.'

'Oh no, we couldn't do that. If you feel you need the artillery, you had better carry on, but the brigadier will require a full explanation first thing in the morning.'

'Of course, that is understood, but tell me, why are you phoning us now, the guns have been firing a good half hour. Surely you must have heard them before?'

'Well, as a matter of fact, there is a bit of a party here tonight to celebrate the end of the war, and more noise than usual.'

'You are a little premature. We will send you an explanation in the morning. Good night.' Vic hung up and rejoined the poker school.

'The B.M. says we may carry on firing,' he announced as he sat down.

Vic chuckled to himself as he prepared for bed. He looked at his watch, the time was a minute to midnight. Overhead the shells whined their comforting sweet music as they went on their way to the Japanese positions.

The next morning started very badly. All patrol reports were sickeningly negative, no Japs had been seen, and no incident occurred. The brigade major had telephoned before breakfast, and again immediatly afterwards, conveying the brigadier's displeasure in no uncertain manner. A general, way back in the rear, had learnt from artillery sources that the 6th Punjabis had, on the previous night, called for several hundred medium and 25-pounder shells, apparently without result and in defiance of a S.E.A.C. order. He had telephoned for an explanation from the brigadier, who at once told his B.M. to get cracking, or words to that effect.

It was a most unpleasant morning. The rain stopped and the sun shone with a fierce heat, and the stink rose from the soil strong and nauseating. There were no dead Japs anywhere, nor any signs of surrender. Vic stalled when the B.M. telephoned, and trying very hard to sound confident said, 'We are waiting for one or two patrol reports to come in. I'll ring you back as soon as possible.'

'Right, but it had better be good, and soon.' The B.M. had rung off abruptly.

Breakfast had been most depressing, for while Vic felt sure of being able, ultimately, to weather the storm which was obviously gathering impetus at brigade, corp, and Army H.Q., it was difficult to find an immediate solution.

If only a few dead Japs had been found at first light. If only there had been some sign, no matter how small, of a surrender before breakfast, everything would have been all right. As it was, the outlook was indeed black. Heads were being demanded, and unless something happened quickly, both the C.O. and Vic were going to have a lot of awkward explaining to do. Vic felt awful, for it was he who had advised the C.O. the night before, and suggested the artillery fire. Fortunately, John did not appear too worried, but Vic had refrained from telling him of the tone of the B.M.'s message, and had only mentioned that the B.M. seemed a bit upset.

'Damn! Damn! Damn!' he muttered to the toast and margarine, his face showing deep consternation, 'what the hell shall we do?'

The B.M. phoned again a few minutes after. 'I take it your report on last night is now ready,' he said almost casually.

'Well, as a matter of fact, it's not quite finished. I'll phone in a few minutes.'

Vic sat down at the table, his face creased in a heavy frown, and his eyes fixed, unseeing, on the situation maps. The telephone bell brought him back to reality.

'Sahib! Sahib!' an excited voice shouted. 'I have got nine Japanese without rifles.'

Vic felt a surge of excitement and his hand trembled a little as he asked the N.C.O. for further details.

A Burman had come across the Old Sittang Channel with a note which he had found pinned to a tree. This was obviously untrue for no sane Burman ever ventured across no-man's land and it was obvious that he had been sent by the Japanese. Two men from the patrol had been sent back to battalion H.Q. with the note, and the local villager had returned. Later, the Japanese appeared without weapons, and indicated as best they could that the war was over, and requested that a British officer be sent to see the Japanese commanding officer. The N.C.O. was apprehensive, and said that, while the nine Japs appeared to be friendly, he felt that it might be a trick and what were his instructions?

'Hold the Japs until we send an officer patrol,' Vic ordered, and congratulated the N.C.O. on his conduct. Most N.C.O.s and officers, for that matter, would, in similar circumstances, probably have shot the nine Japs and asked questions afterwards. In restraining his men, the Naik had displayed great courage. His action undoubtedly hastened the subsequent cease fire.

Vic immediately appreciated the real significance of the message, but he sat a moment, motionless beside the telephone. Then he grabbed the receiver and bawled to the operator.

'Get me brigade, quick!'

While the call was coming through, Vic reported to the C.O. who at once gave orders for Major Mike Boon to take a full strength platoon of Sikhs to the forward platoon base.

The brigade major was delighted when Vic passed the

information concerning the nine unarmed Japs and the request for a meeting, and, after a minute's delay while he apparently consulted with his brigadier, he ordered that the Japanese should be despatched to Brigade H.Q. immediately. He emphasised the importance of keeping the Japs in custody.

But a telephone call to Posabe revealed that the Japs had already gone. They had decided to return to their own village. The patrol leader was almost in tears, but he couldn't be blamed, and Vic, annoyed and disappointed as he was, did not reprimand him. Immediately the doubts came flooding back. The Japs were not going to surrender, and the jubilation which had swept through Pyabyo a short time ago once again gave way to gloom.

Vic telephoned brigade. 'Those Japanese, the prisoners, they're gone,' he said tersely.

'Gone? What do you mean?' The B.M. demanded angrily. 'I told you to detain them.'

'They decided to go back to their position. What do you suggest we should have done, shot them?' Vic was getting nettled and his voice was belligerent.

'Hold the line a moment,' the B.M. said, and Vic waited, swearing violently to himself.

The B.M.'s voice came through the ear-phone quietly. 'The brigadier wishes to speak to your C.O.'

The brigadier's remarks were pointed but there was no answer to Vic's suggestion of shooting the Japanese. No one could suggest what other action the Naik* could have taken to keep the Japs in custody. Had he used force, the first opportunity to negotiate the surrender would have been lost, perhaps for a very long time. His position, too, was quite near to a heavily defended village, and undoubtedly the use of force against the nine unarmed Japs would have brought strong retaliation.

The departure of the nine Japanese soldiers was depressing, and once again, John, the C.O. was worried. 'Damn it,' he said, 'we have nothing to show. No surrender, and now no prisoners. The brigadier is less than happy.' But there was some hope. Mike Boon was on his way to meet the Japanese, and whilst his mission had been initiated on the flimsiest of information, it was hopeful.

*The rank Naik is equivalent to that of Corporal.

The note from the Japanese arrived just in time; Pyabyo was over-run, not by the Japanese but by British generals and their staff who, apparently, came to reprove. The arrival of the note changed everything; the evidence was now that the war was over. No one in the battalion was congratulated on hastening the surrender but there were no reprimands for using the artillery on the previous night. In a crowd of senior officers, one staff officer murmured to Vic, 'you are lucky to have got away with it. I shudder to think what would have happened to you and your C.O. if the Japs had not contacted you.'

'Next time,' Vic quipped, 'we will do it differently.'

Meanwhile, Major Mike Boon was heading east toward Posabe on foot with thirty Sikhs to the patrol's position, where he was soon joined by the brigade intelligence officer and an interpreter. Mike was the senior officer and on him rested an enormous responsibility. He knew the Jap and never for one moment believed that a mass surrender was possible, neither did anyone else in the area of Pyabyo. His orders had been to investigate and to accept the surrender should an opportunity occur.

The party moved across the open country and halted on the near side of the Sittang Old Channel. The Japanese party could be seen on the far bank standing in the open quite casually, but with an armed party of about thirty soldiers in close attendance. Two of them made their way through the water, and slowly approached Mike's party. The time was 1430 hours and the date was 23 August.

Apart from the two Japanese trudging steadily through the water, no one moved. No one spoke. There was a tense, hushed atmosphere.

Mike returned the enemy soldier's salute and listened to their message: 'Would the British officers meet the Japanese officer *on the other side* of the river?'

Instantly, suspicion arose, and John and Vic listening in at H.Q. decided that it was a trap. John said to Mike, 'Tell the bloody Jap that you decline his request and that if he does not cross the water by 1600 hours there will be no parley.'

Mike sent the message to the Japanese officer and received a reply suggesting that the Japanese party and the British party should both start walking toward each other at 1500 hours. Thus, his face was saved, and at the appointed hour the parties met in the shallow water of the old channel. Friend and foe stood together. The war was really over.

The Japanese lieutenant was courteous but not servile, and at once requested that the British should stop firing. He made no mention of surrender, and for a few moments the British representatives felt at a loss but Mike quickly recovered, and queried the Japanese intentions, to which the lieutenant replied in English with a slight American accent that in three days the Japanese would withdraw to Moulmein to embark for Japan, and his only request was that the British would please stop the artillery shelling.

It was evident that it was not the right time to mention the word surrender, so Mike and his colleague wrote a message to the O.C. Nippon Army, Nyaungkashe-Mokpalin area, requesting that a senior Japanese officer should meet a senior British officer at the forward Japanese railway position. The enemy officer promised to arrange a meeting.

'Thank God for that,' Vic said to John in the battalion command post, where both had been listening in to Mike's wireless commentary.

'I can't help thinking that if the Jap hadn't contacted us we would have received an awful rocket from brigade,' John replied.

'Heavens, yes, I had clean forgotten about that report they were asking for this morning. Anyway, I couldn't care less now. John, old boy,' Vic cried jubilantly, grasping John's hand, 'the war is over, to hell with reports. Let's have a drink.'

So, at 1700 hours on 23 August 1945, four buglers stood on a high patch of ground in the village of Pyabyo, faced outwards, and sounded the cease fire. In the mess, the officers gave a toast to themselves.

The cease fire was unofficial and next morning the battalion was again in disgrace. In the excitement of the previous day, Johnny Loosemore had been forgotten. He had disappeared but had been most active. His account of the parley with the Japs, the first sign of surrender, was exclusive to him alone, and using a method known only to himself, he had sent or taken it to Rangoon for transmission to the U.K. By so doing, he had bypassed brigade, corps, and army headquarters. Someone, probably a security officr at Rangoon, decided to refer the report to Army H.Q. and next morning the battalion were reminded in no uncertain terms of various Army Orders relating to the activities of war correspondents and security.

The message came during breakfast, when the brigadier was about to meet a Japanese senior officer at the railway rendezvous. Vic opened the envelope, read the message carefully, folded it back to its original shape, and without changing his expression, resumed eating his toast.

'What a damn cheek,' he thought, 'we finish off the damn war, and then get a rocket for not keeping it secret. I suppose Johnnie's report should have been vetted, but what the hell! I forgot all about him. Anyway, it was a good effort on his part. He will get a rocket too. Pity. I wonder what would have happened if the report had slipped past the censor, and the news had been published in the U.K. before it was public knowledge in Burma and India!'

On his return to the command post, Jemadar Bashir Ahmed placed a pile of letters for signature on the trestle table.

'What's this, Jemadar Sahib? Why so many copies of the note from the Japanese?' asked Vic.

'Well, sir, I thought perhaps you may wish to give a copy to every officer. I thought it would perhaps make an interesting souvenir,' he said, choosing his words with care.

Vic suddenly felt very tired and without thought for the time of day he lay down on his bed beside the table. He held the letter up to the light so that he could read it easily. But it slipped from his fingers and fluttered to the floor. When the Jemadar came in five minutes later, Vic was sound asleep, his face pale and looking utterly exhausted.

He awoke three hours later, picked up the letter and read it:

ATTENTION!

Burmese!

My Friend,

Here, I must tell you as you know, that the war is over. We Japanese Army won't do any harm to you as long as you won't shoot. May be you might say it isn't us. Well all right whoever it is tell them also about this.

If you want to come into your village leave the weapon

behind. While you are carrying it we will think you are hoping resistance.

It means danger!

Come! We will gladly have a talk with you and help you all we can.

Don't be afraid, let us understand each other. I know how you need your house goods. I swear those without weapons are allowed to come into any village. This goes to any races.

I hope somebody can read this. The man who have read this please come to my place with this letter. I am starving knowledge.

Remember no weapons are allowed coming into your village.

Sincerely Yours
One of the Japanese Officer
??????????
At the Thabyegon Village

Three months later, John and Vic were sitting in the mess tent, a large splendid affair with a blue lining. It was nearly midday and they were drinking coffee, and talking to a Japanese major who was in charge of the working party which came every day to do fatigues for the 6th Punjabis.

'You must admit that your army were well and truly beaten,' John said provocatively.

'Of course not, the Imperial Nippon Army will never be defeated.'

'You are talking absolute nonsense. If you are not defeated, then why are you here? Why do you do all our dirty fatigues, make our football ground, and why did you give up your arms?'

The Japanese officer drew himself up.

'We,' he paused, 'are soldiers of our His Imperial Highness, the Emperor of Japan, and, therefore, obey all his orders without question. He gave his armies orders, with which we complied. That is all.' His eyes blinked behind his thick glasses, and his face was impassive, solemn and serious.

'Oh, come now,' John taunted him, 'that is bosh, and if it is true, what would you do now if your precious emperor gave the order to start fighting again?'

'We would fight,' the Jap officer said.

'But what with? You haven't any arms or supplies. What would you do?'

'We would make clubs from branches of trees and attack you at once. If necessary, we would kill you with our bare hands. We would then seize your weapons and release our prisoners. The Japanese Imperial Nippon Army is never beaten. Our army was ordered to capture Burma in 1942, now we have been ordered to stop fighting, but the Emperor of Japan is supreme, and above all human beings. His word will always be obeyed. We have had a four year fighting war which is finished; now we will have a trade war for the next ninety six years. You will see.'

The Japanese major spoke passionately in a high voice, clipping his words short. He saluted jerkily, with a flourish, and stalked away, head held high.

John and Vic watched him disappear into the jungle in silence. Then Vic said, 'I say John, be a bit more careful. He was damn serious. Don't for heaven's sake start another war.'

For the historians –
The first atomic bomb fell on Hiroshima on 6 August 1945.
The second, and let us pray the last, fell on Nagasaki on 9 August 1945.
The Allied terms were accepted on 15 August 1945.
The Japanese Emperor issued an edict ordering the Japanese armed forces to surrender on 15 August 1945.